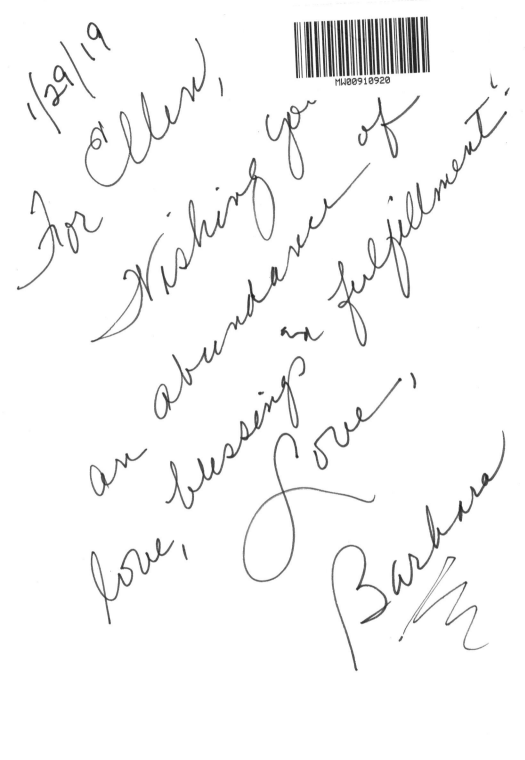

1/29/19

For Ellen,

Wishing you
an abundance of
blessings an fulfillment.

love,

Love,

Barbara

"*Before You Love Again* is filled with wisdom and practicality, presented in simple, easy-to-follow advice. Barbara Tucciarone has used her personal and professional expertise to create a classic recipe for living your life healed and whole. I am delighted to recommend this book, not just for those who are recovering from divorce, but for anyone who wants to improve their present marriage. "Lo Anne Mayer, author of Celestial Conversations: Healing Relationships After Death

Love 'n Light,
Lo Anne

www.celestialconversations.com
www.internationalgriefcouncil.org

Please support the GoFundMe effort for the International Grief Council
https://www.gofundme.com/finding-hope-after-loss

BARBARA S. TUCCIARONE, PSYD

Before You
Love
Again

BALBOA.
PRESS
A DIVISION OF HAY HOUSE

Balboa Press books may be ordered through booksellers or by contacting:

Balboa Press
A Division of Hay House
1663 Liberty Drive
Bloomington, IN 47403
www.balboapress.com
1 (877) 407-4847

Because of the dynamic nature of the Internet, any web addresses or links contained in this book may have changed since publication and may no longer be valid. The views expressed in this work are solely those of the author and do not necessarily reflect the views of the publisher, and the publisher hereby disclaims any responsibility for them.

The author of this book does not dispense medical advice or prescribe the use of any technique as a form of treatment for physical, emotional, or medical problems without the advice of a physician, either directly or indirectly. The intent of the author is only to offer information of a general nature to help you in your quest for emotional and spiritual well-being. In the event you use any of the information in this book for yourself, which is your constitutional right, the author and the publisher assume no responsibility for your actions.

Any people depicted in stock imagery provided by Getty Images are models, and such images are being used for illustrative purposes only. Certain stock imagery © Getty Images.

This book is a work of non-fiction. Unless otherwise noted, the author and the publisher make no explicit guarantees as to the accuracy of the information contained in this book and in some cases, names of people and places have been altered to protect their privacy.

Print information available on the last page.

ISBN: 978-1-9822-0092-3 (sc)
ISBN: 978-1-9822-0094-7 (hc)
ISBN: 978-1-9822-0093-0 (e)

Library of Congress Control Number: 2018903774

Balboa Press rev. date: 08/15/2018

Contents

It's not what happens to you, but how you react to it that matters.

—Epictetus (AD 55-c. 135)

Dedication

This book is dedicated to my husband, Stephen, my cherished, loving and devoted best friend and partner. Without his encouragement and support, this book would not have been written.

B.S.T.

Prologue

Throughout the years, I have gathered a wealth of information both from my research and from my colleagues. The wonderful clients I have worked with over the years, in addition to receiving my own experiences in coaching and guiding people on relationships, have provided me with more precious information than I could have gathered just from books. When I went through the difficult and painful process of ending my own thirteen-year marriage, I had three young boys I was struggling to support while finishing up my master's degree. I remember it all too well. I felt as if I were struggling to keep my head above water while a weight was dragging me down. It was the most challenging experience of my entire life, as everything that was precious to me changed on a dime.

Eventually, after my healing process was complete, I successfully remarried. I used my knowledge not only to empower myself but also to teach and coach others to create happy, fulfilling new relationships with the tools provided in this book, which I will now share with you, the reader. This book contains how-tos.

We live in a society that promotes happiness, success, and optimism. When we encounter a devastating loss, there are few customs or rituals to help us find closure and deal with and complete our feelings of sadness, emptiness, and loss.

Many people look to numb their feelings. It can be tempting to find distractions from processing these painful feelings. We keep busy, we work harder and longer, we go on shopping sprees, or we find other ways to push down those painful feelings. Of course, there are a variety of mood-altering and sweet treats and other temptations to distract us, but these forms of escape do not lead to a healthy resolution of our feelings or to spiritual growth. The astonishing truth is that 67 percent of second and third relationships end in divorce. It takes time and knowledge to heal our emotional wounds. There are no effective painkillers to heal these wounds. Alcohol, drugs, food, sex, and so on will mask the symptoms temporarily, but in the long run, they will only make matters worse. This book will provide the reader with the tools to heal feelings, attain closure, find peace, and see all the gifts provided by the former relationship. It is my hope that this book will help you, the reader, to move beyond blame and anger and clear the way for a new life to begin.

> Adversity, every failure, every heartache carries with it the seed of an equal or greater benefit.
>
> —Napoleon Hill

It has been said that you can't have a beginning without an ending. The staggering number of second, third, and fourth divorces is attributable to all the people who did not know the necessity of becoming complete regarding their past relationship(s) before entering new ones.

Feelings of rage, anger, blame, frustration, sadness, self-pity, guilt, and remorse, to name a few, are all painful and difficult to reconcile and resolve. However difficult it is, you must resolve your feelings if you are to close the door completely on the old and be able to create a new and lasting relationship. Otherwise, you will continue to repeat your mistakes. In our society, it is not common to have the skills to heal emotionally. We need to get past the anger and blame, which will help us move into the sadness of mourning the loss of the relationship. It is necessary to grieve. Facing feelings that make us feel vulnerable is necessary if we are to heal and release our emotional baggage. Otherwise, that baggage will contaminate the new relationship somewhere down the road. It could take weeks, months, or years, but it will without a doubt rear its head when least expected.

Jennifer came into my office one morning. It was apparent she had been crying. She said, "I'm so upset that twenty-two years of my life went into the garbage. I spent twenty-two miserable years with Howie. I wasted so much time with someone who wasn't right for me! Why didn't I get out sooner? I'm so angry and frustrated. I'm just so miserable!"

Why We Avoid Endings

Have you ever felt this way? Self-awareness is the key to creating inner peace, happiness, and heightened self-confidence. Once you have achieved this, you will attract and create the next healthy, fulfilling relationship. You will need to approach the past by neutralizing your feelings regarding your former spouse. It is equally important to understand the part you played in the death of the old relationship. By becoming indifferent and emotionally detached, you will be able to see the gifts you received from the old relationship. Eventually, you might even be able to wish your ex happiness and joy as you focus your life on moving forward and loving again.

To move on, it is essential that we are complete. This might sound like a simple, quick, and easy task, but it is not. Consider that most people have not attained their emotional divorce. They still refer to their exes as "my wife" or "my husband." They find reasons to enjoy social activities together and find pleasurable activities to share as they pour new energy into the old relationship to keep it going. This is the same as constantly picking at a scab: every time the healing is beginning, the person completely picks at and pulls off the newly formed scab, prolonging the healing process. This is a distraction from facing the painful emotions of saying goodbye. Continuing this togetherness is like adding Miracle-Gro to a plant that has died. However, there are many couples who are ambivalent about letting go and moving forward. There are also couples who choose to do work on their ambivalence in coaching or counseling sessions. When feelings of love or attachment exist, it is first necessary to determine if the relationship can be saved or repaired or if the best choice is to close the chapter and move on.

Research bears out the extraordinarily high rate of second and third marriages ending in divorce. One of the major reasons is that one or both did not let go and did not focus their intentions on true healing. Only resolving the difficult feelings will ultimately lead to neutrality and heightened self-awareness.

Personal growth and self-awareness are important by-products of this effort. Attaining a healthy level of neutrality means that we are no longer hooked into fighting and wasting our precious energy. We take back our power and refrain from getting into power struggles. When we have obtained our emotional divorce, we have chosen to be happy rather than right. We can respond with logic rather than emotion. As we grow in our understanding of what happened and what our part was, we develop wisdom along with compassion, both for ourselves and for our former partners. Eventually, we even start to notice the gifts the relationship provided. Closing the door to the old and inviting in the new sounds easy, but it requires using the tools found in later chapters.

Dr. Holly Hein, relationship expert and author, states in her popular book *Sexual Detours* that five to ten years post-divorce, 33 percent of men admit to still being angry at their exes. Sadly, 50 percent of women are still angry as well. Wow! Can you imagine spending five to ten years after a divorce or separation still feeling angry? Some people are spending approximately 10 percent of their lives being angry. It is no wonder then that the statistics for subsequent relationships are so dismal. Approximately 50 percent of first marriages and 67 percent of second marriages end in divorce.

Furthermore, the statistics reveal that the divorce rate for third and fourth marriages is even higher.

When we do the necessary work of attaining closure and getting complete, we create an opportunity for personal and emotional growth. To be healed will translate into emotional freedom, which means we will no longer be holding on to the anger, blame, and bitterness of our past relationship. By attaining a healthy level of neutrality, we will be empowered to let go of the past. We will no longer be reacting to the triggers that have previously led to so much bitterness and anger.

Self-awareness is the key to creating inner peace, happiness, and heightened self-confidence, which allows you to attract and create your next healthy, fulfilling relationship. You must approach the past by becoming neutral regarding your former partner. This will provide you with the opportunity to understand the contributions you made to the death of the former relationship. Once you become emotionally detached, you will be able to see the many gifts you received from the old relationship. Eventually, you might be able to wish your ex happiness and joy as you focus your life on moving forward and loving again. That is when you know you are healed.

In her popular book *The Good Divorce*, Dr. Constance Ahrons writes, "For most people ending a marriage is the most traumatic decision of their life. Transitions are turning points. They're uncomfortable periods that mark the beginning of something new while signifying the ending of something familiar."

In the end, just three things matter: How well we have lived. How well we have loved. How well we have learned to let go.
—Jack Kornfield, PhD

Chapter 1

It Takes Two to Tango

A key factor in being able to love again is whether or not a person has attained self-awareness. It is all too easy and tempting to point an accusatory finger and blame the other for the death of the relationship. However, it takes two to make a relationship, and it also takes two to break it. Frequently, people become stuck and harbor thoughts of blame, such as the following:

"She was a crazy bitch!"
"He was a lazy good-for-nothing!"
"She was cold and uncaring!"
"He had an outrageous temper!"
"She put her career ahead of everyone!"
"He was emotionally unavailable!"
"She lied constantly!"
"He was a womanizer!"

These are common accusations people hold on to regarding their exes. Blaming the other prevents us from being accountable. However, when we are accountable, we grow and move forward.

For starters, I ask my clients, "What was it in you that attracted that type of personality?" That question is often met with "I don't know. I guess I'm just unlucky in love." It is important to realize that both parties contributed to the breakdown in trust and closeness. It is necessary to understand the baggage that each carried into the relationship. Consider the following:

1. Were there deep issues with control?
2. Were there core issues with abandonment?
3. Were there core issues with rejection?

While these are deep underlying subconscious issues, it is necessary to identify what *your* core issues were. What were your needs at the beginning of the relationship? What are your needs now? What is your communication style? Would it be helpful to work on your communication style? (See chapter 11.) The challenge is to understand what part you played in the breakup of the relationship. Every relationship provides important life lessons. We can choose to learn them now or learn them from the next relationship.

It truly does take two to create a successful relationship, just as it takes two to end a relationship. If you are willing to accept your part of the responsibility, you will greatly increase the chances that your next relationship will be healthy, happy, and satisfying.

Frank entered coaching with the complaint that his estranged wife had an outrageous temper. He often referred to her as "that crazy bitch." She would fly off the handle during discussions, call him despicable names, and even throw things at him. She not only cursed at him but also frequently cursed at their two daughters. Frank and the girls lived a highly stressed existence, trying not to get her angry, as she would explode and "go off the rails." The three of them felt as if they had to walk on eggshells. The anger, disrespect, and hostility were so intense that all three were on pins and needles, expecting the worst at any moment. During the two-year divorce process, Frank met another woman. Frank's new love interest spent most weekends living with Frank and the girls at his new house. It turned out that she too had a violent temper, and she was as self-centered and demanding as Frank's estranged wife.

Once Frank saw how both women were emotionally identical to his mother and sister, he reassessed his relationship. Frank was willing to do the inner work to change his old self-limiting beliefs. In his coaching sessions, he chose to work on increasing his self-esteem and improving his issues of low self-worth. Not only did he get a successful divorce, but he also ended the relationship with the second woman. At that time, Frank chose to deliberately spend time alone, processing his feelings while continuing to work on himself. He learned how to identify feelings and how to express his needs while finding new interests and hobbies that filled him with joy. It wasn't his fault that he had grown up the son of a volatile and angry mother. He chose to never again walk on eggshells and fix another "broken" woman. He realized he deserved a partner who was his emotional equal. Frank regained his self-worth, found happiness, and enjoyed his new self-awareness.

Like Frank, once you reach this point, you will need to resolve feelings of remorse and conflict. The sadness will have either lessened or been healed. The confusion around what happened will have morphed into a heightened understanding of cause and effect. Having a new state of consciousness will enable you to see what part you played in the death of your relationship. Ultimately, you will move in the direction of having an appreciation for the gifts the relationship provided. You will have become more enlightened, optimistic, and hopeful at the end of the journey of feeling and completion.

Yesterday is history.
Tomorrow is a mystery.
Today is a gift.
That's why we call it the present.

Healing time allows us to reflect on who we are as unique, deserving human beings. What are our values, what are our priorities, and what do we really need to make us happy? This can be a delicious time of discovering who we are down deep inside.

As we continue to evolve and learn more about ourselves, we can discover the answers to these key questions:

- What are the priorities in my life?
- What brings me joy?
- What am I proudest of?
- What are my values?
- What do I need to be happy?
- Am I an optimist or a pessimist?
- Am I an initiator or a responder?
- What am I passionate about?
- What are my hot buttons?

- What are my lifetime goals? Ideally, where would I like to see myself in two, five, and ten years?
- Who are my closest friends? Do I connect with them on a regular basis?
- Who gives me support?
- How comfortable am I asking for support when I need it?
- Do I consider myself to be nonjudgmental?
- Am I compassionate?
- Am I a kind and loving person?
- Am I thoughtful and considerate?
- Do I say what I mean and mean what I say?
- Am I flexible?
- Am I able to ask for help when I need it?
- Am I able to say no to others?
- Is it easy for me to acknowledge when I'm wrong?
- Am I able to say I'm sorry?
- Am I sincere?
- Am I dependable?
- Am I respectful?
- Am I respectable?
- What are the ways I show kindness to others?
- What are the ways I show kindness to myself?

Many people have attained success in their careers. However, achieving success in a relationship requires different skill sets. It is necessary to have self-awareness, excellent communication skills, and compassion with positive expectations. The willingness to compromise is essential. If we haven't a clue as to the role we played in the relationship, we will bring the same behavior and self-limiting beliefs forward, repeating the patterns.

Take Amanda, for example. She would bend over backward trying to please her partner, giving in to his many requests to keep the peace. She was admittedly fearful of disagreeing, hated confrontations, and hated conflict. Her avoidance behavior resulted in her continuously yielding to Brad's numerous expectations. Amanda did not consider what it was that *she* wanted and needed, as it did not occur to her to speak up, be assertive, and compromise when their needs did not match. Amanda worked long hours at her law firm and looked forward to a two-week break at the shore, where she could just be.

She and Brad had discussed this plan months earlier. Brad, on the other hand, became enthusiastic about planning a trip to Europe with another couple he knew from his college days. After finalizing the European plans, Brad announced his proclamation regarding "their" trip to Europe. Amanda stopped herself from saying that she needed a mental-health break from all the stress at work and needed a more tranquil vacation that would help her regroup. Inwardly, she was hoping to discuss their plans, but she didn't say any of that. Instead, she reluctantly went along with Brad's plans, telling herself that it was just easier to do things his way. Unconsciously, she harbored a truckload of resentments. On the second day of their European trip, Amanda had an accident and broke her leg in two places. While she was lying in the hospital, recovering from surgery, she thought, *Well, I'm finally going to be able to relax and do nothing for the rest of my vacation.* At that point, Amanda became aware of her pattern of putting Brad's needs ahead of hers and always accepting the role of a people pleaser. Suddenly, she became aware that not only was her body giving her a wakeup call, but she was also now crystal clear about wanting to change her long-standing pattern of putting others first at the expense of her own fulfillment.

She'd been focused on others and neglectful of her own needs and happiness. She chose to sign up for coaching sessions, primarily to work on this pattern. Amanda was committed to making herself her number-one priority as she put the principles of self-love and self-care in motion. During her coaching sessions, she recognized that this pattern extended to her friends, family, and past relationships as well. As she grew and discovered her identity, she found her life more satisfying and pleasing. She became more comfortable with herself and more comfortable around others. She became increasingly creative and energized, experiencing bursts of joy when she placed her priorities first. She began a program of excellent self-care that began with biking, yoga, and meditation. She was so thrilled at her new outlook on life and the new person she had become that she referred her clients, colleagues, and friends to make appointments for life coaching.

> We don't meet people by accident. They are meant to cross our path for a reason.
> —Kathryn Perez

A Good Divorce Is Better Than a Bad Marriage

You have heard it said that the opposite of love is hate. Not really! The opposite of love is indifference.

Anger, resentment, blame, and guilt can greatly contribute to unhappiness and stress. We cannot be our best when we are dealing with stress. These feelings of anger, blame, and retaliation often hide our emotional pain.

Recent research has identified a correlation between chronic anger, hostility, and a lack of forgiveness. This blend results in tension and defensiveness, which blocks the positive energy we need to feel good about ourselves.

When we have strong negative emotions and feelings toward someone, there is an energy connection. It might be bad energy, but it is energy nonetheless. This energy connection binds two people together. It is like two magnets drawing power from one another. We all know how draining and exhausting it feels to be in the presence of someone who upsets us and who is negative and oppositional. After spending time with that person, we feel depleted and sometimes even depressed. Our energy has been drained. It can be the same for us when we are interacting with our ex. If we harbor old blame and resentments, we cannot let go and move on. We are not free.

We can only grow emotionally if we become more and more self-aware by choosing to let go and forgive. The uplifting freedom we feel when we choose to release the past is palpable. (See chapter 8, "Forgiveness.") When we strive to become neutral, we take our power back and can enjoy the present. Whether we choose to be happy or unhappy, the choice is ours to make!

When we go with the flow and are open to everything that happens to us, we learn that every problem offers us opportunities to grow. When we choose to be receptive to the gifts the universe gives us, we gain wisdom and become empowered and self-aware.

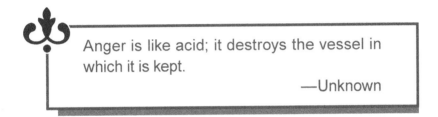

> Anger is like acid; it destroys the vessel in which it is kept.
>
> —Unknown

Closure will prepare the way for a new happy, healthy, beneficial relationship. For example, when Donna first came to see me, she was full of anger, blame, and rage. She was feeling hurt and confused.

At first, she blamed Colin for their breakup and for refusing counseling. As time passed, Donna chose to stop blaming Colin for being alone and having to deal with all the facets of life without him. She no longer put herself in a victim position, which was draining her energy and reducing her self-worth. Eventually, Donna wrote Colin several letters (which were not mailed), expressing angry, ambivalent, and sad feelings as she mourned the end of her marriage and partnership with Colin. After processing her feelings, the next stage for Donna was one of finding out who she was as a separate and unique person. Donna started ballroom dancing, joined a book club, and began volunteering at a local animal shelter. She even adopted a dog, which she had yearned to do for a long time. As a matter of fact, when she was at the vet's office with her new four-legged friend, she met a man with the same breed as hers, and they began chatting. It turned out that Mike lived two blocks away from her childhood home, loved ballroom dancing, and was an avid reader. Donna began a relationship with Mike about two years after her divorce was finalized, and they developed a friendship. Donna concluded that when we come from a good place, good things mirror themselves back at us. The universe sends people into our lives who reflect the signals we put out. We attract people who are on the same emotional wavelength. I had the opportunity to meet Mike on several occasions and congratulated them both on having built a healthy and fulfilling relationship. It is amazing what happens when we live fully and happily in the present moment and give up the ghosts from the past.

Thus, the reason for this book is to understand the process of letting go and learn the steps to reach an indifferent state. Perhaps you will even wish your partner well and truly mean it. It is imperative that you learn to be complete and realize that whatever you went through was a precious gift, a learning experience, and something to be grateful for.

Remember, you have become a more experienced, richer, and wiser person for having invested in your former relationship, even if that relationship came to a painful end.

Every experience we have makes us more aware of what our emotional needs and values are. In other words, we have an opportunity to know what we want as well as what we do not want and when we want it.

Sarah came into my office one day. Her goal was to process some deep feelings of anger and resentment. Joel had walked out on her, telling her he wanted some space and wasn't sure if he was the "marrying type." Within the month, Sarah had discovered that Joel was replacing her with a woman who lived in the neighborhood. Shortly after the woman had become a widow, Joel, playing the role of good neighbor, had volunteered to help this woman with several house repairs. Eventually, Sarah discovered that Joel had become intimate with this neighbor. This caused Sarah to question her own self-worth and value. Sarah came to understand the necessity of moving past blame and anger and was willing to do the inner work to get past her feelings of shock, hurt, depression, and blame.

As Sarah progressed in her coaching sessions, she began to see the entire picture more clearly. (This is like standing next to a train wreck and trying to understand what just happened and how it happened.) In retrospect, Sarah could see the origins of many lifelong patterns. She referred to it as "taking a journey within."

Sarah and Joel had started their relationship while he was still married to his first wife. Joel, at age eighteen, ran away from a highly dysfunctional family. There were high levels of abuse as well as neglect. He chose to attend a college that was three thousand miles away. Once he completed college, he totally disconnected from his family of origin— not just his mother and father but also his three siblings. Joel had deep-seated fears of closeness and dependency.

Sarah also looked at her own life's patterns, and it turned out she had also grown up with two dysfunctional parents. Both were addicted to alcohol as well as other escapism behaviors, such as avoidance and chronic lying. Sarah's role in the family was to try to "fix" Mom by becoming a surrogate mother and taking on the caretaker role. During her teenage years, Sarah cooked the meals, helped the younger kids with their homework, made their lunches, did laundry for the entire family, and felt it was up to her to hold the family together.

Mom was often the victim of Dad's physical and verbal abuse, while Sarah tried to protect both Mom and the kids from Dad. Once she was old enough to drive, it became her job to pick up her inebriated father from the country club. Sarah spoke of how guilty she felt when she began attending a local college—it was the one time she'd done something that was entirely for herself. For a long time, she had been too busy taking care of everyone else to have friends or even date. During her time at college, there was a family crisis. Her brother was killed while driving in an intoxicated state. Her mother suggested that perhaps she could go to college "later on" and come home to help out. Sarah went to a counselor at school and mustered up the courage to tell her mother no. She needed to finish her nursing degree. For her entire life, Sarah had put her needs last while being outer-focused. In the first year of Sarah's employment, while working for a physician, she met Joel, a patient at the office. She was immediately impressed by his blue eyes, flattery, and happy-go-lucky manner.

For several months, they had a flirtatious relationship. Joel told her how abusive his wife was due to her dependence on prescription drugs. She was moody, abusive, and explosive and kept telling him, "Get out!" Sarah saw Joel as someone to "fix." This was a man who was stuck in a destructive relationship with a mean, disrespectful, detached wife. In a short time, Joel moved into Sarah's apartment. Looking back on it all, Sarah noticed several significant red flags. When she was ready to do her own inner work, she realized it was time to focus on herself. Focusing only on others had resulted in her not knowing what *she* needed to be happy. In finally thinking about her own needs, she could become self-aware and begin the inner healing journey necessary for personal growth. Sarah realized she had never mourned the death of her younger brother. This was a perfect place to begin, as she realized she also needed to mourn the lack of family, since her family had not provided the safety, structure, and love needed by all children. She ultimately learned how to give herself the support and nurturing that had been denied her while growing up.

She connected the dots and realized the anger, rage, loneliness, and betrayal she felt toward Joel were feelings that had begun a long time ago. This was the perfect time to heal so much pain. Her primary core values were respect, loyalty, honesty, compassion, and kindness. She realized how important they were to honor the unique person she was. She would not compromise her values again to make someone else happy. Additionally, she created a list of what was acceptable as well as what was unacceptable in a significant relationship.

Throughout the years, Sarah has continued to keep in touch with me by e-mail. She is now living with a partner who has values identical to hers and who is a great match in terms of her acceptable and unacceptable behaviors.

She learned to get in touch with the beautiful person who existed within, regained her confidence, and developed interests and close friends. She changed to a much more rewarding and lucrative career as a medical sales representative, one that afforded her much success. Sarah had come a long way, from a woman who tried to please everyone to a woman who excelled and learned to please herself.

Chapter 2

Getting Your Emotional Divorce

Most people do not know how to get their emotional divorce. For healing to occur, it is not enough to just put a Band-Aid on the wound; it is vital to truly understand what happened in the former relationship. Healing needs to occur without blame or judgment, as those behaviors will only poison the wound. Healing must be done with understanding and compassion. First, begin by showing compassion for yourself.

For the healing to begin and to attain closure, it is necessary to bury the old relationship. When a relationship dies, it is painful and sad. I want you to think about going to a funeral. People are expected to grieve and mourn; many show up to offer support and encouragement. They offer help, love, and hope to the bereft spouse.

Often, there is much sympathy, kindness, understanding, and help offered to the widow or widower. Loss is a dramatic, life-changing event. Divorce, like death, is a terrifying and dramatic life change. Research has shown that divorce can be even more devastating emotionally than a death. You find yourself suddenly alone; you have no one to share your thoughts, dreams, and even frustrations with. You are, for all intents and purposes, a widow or widower. You are fragile at this stage of uncoupling.

As Dr. Christiane Northrup, author of *Making Life Easy: A Simple Guide to a Divinely Inspired Life,* explains,

> Heartbreak can cause clinical depression. In fact, research shows that losses impacting self-esteem such as a breakup, are twice as likely to trigger depression versus ones that involve loss alone, such as death. Part of this stems from the fact that relationships change the way we think about ourselves. Heartbreak due to a romantic break-up or divorce can leave you questioning your identity.

Dr. Northrup goes on to explain that during stress and heartbreak, the brain pumps the body full of cortisol and epinephrine, two chemicals that can be damaging to the body. Additionally, these chemicals can affect the quality of our sleep, the way we think, and the way we feel about ourselves.

When we experience the deep pain caused by betrayal, loss, or rejection, the pain is so powerful that we might feel as if our heart is breaking.

Dr. Steven Sinatra, cardiologist and author of *Heartbreak and Heart Disease*, has conducted invaluable research on the physical effects of heartbreak. In his popular book, he writes about what can happen to your heart after the sudden, unexpected loss of an important connection. He describes how stress hormones can cause physical symptoms, including the death of heart cells, which is called necrosis. He has concluded that not only is heartbreak a threat to your health, but also, a devastating loss can lead to a breakdown of the heart functions. In some cases, heartbreak has been reported to have caused strokes or heart attacks. The American Heart Association has a term for the physical effects of heartbreak: broken-heart syndrome.

When you're left to fend for yourself, it is imperative that you turn inward. You've just had the equivalent of open-heart surgery; you're into the earliest phase of healing your broken heart. You need to give yourself the time, compassion, patience, and kindness you would give to your best friend or a child suffering a major loss.

In death, there is no choice but to accept the finality of the situation. Loss hurts! It can provoke an extraordinarily high level of anxiety. The same emotional dynamics exist with a divorce; however, in addition to the loss of one's partner and all that loss entails, most cases require an intense discussion and settlement about future arrangements for children, property and other asset distributions, living arrangements, holidays, friends, in-laws, and even pets. To add to the huge pileup of stressful matters, often, there is a change in the new financial situation of each partner. These are numerous complications that the death of a partner does not bring.

There are many strong and contradictory feelings that need to be resolved. Otherwise, if we sweep these strong feelings under the rug, they will simply resurface. Consider a beach ball. If we push the beach ball down under the water, it will pop up somewhere else. In the same way, the anger will continue to resurface. Letting the air out of the beach ball and then releasing it will be the choice that yields the completion of dealing with the old anger.

Aimee met John while she was newly separated. They truly hit it off—lots of delicious chemistry. They found one another fascinating and felt they could talk about an infinite number of topics. They became a committed couple in a short time. Within months of the finalization of Aimee's divorce, they married. Within the first year, this new couple began bickering over seemingly small differences that ultimately led to disappointment, sadness, hopelessness, and frustration, to say the least. As Aimee stated in one of her coaching sessions, "I initially felt that John was my best friend. We had a great thing going, but in a short time, everything started going downhill. It seems that now we argue about everything. We wind up not speaking to each other for hours or even days. This is happening more and more, and I'm heartbroken to think we might not make it. We both agree that we love one another. It's all so confusing." Aimee had not completed her emotional divorce. She was now displacing a great deal of anger onto John. Both Aimee and John had no clue what they had contributed to the failure of their first marriages. Both still needed to resolve old negative feelings from the past.

It is imperative to mourn the loss of someone you were once in love with—someone you had invested in. Mourning the loss of broken dreams takes knowhow, patience, and time. Additionally, there is a huge change when we go from "we" to "I." This is the time to discover who you truly are and what's most important in your life with a positive outlook toward the future. By understanding how important it is to grieve the loss of a loved one, we can complete and heal. This interim phase creates in us a sense of vulnerability as we process many feelings during the letting-go phase. It is normal to have feelings of sadness, anxiety and loneliness due to an ending; however, we can learn from everything that happened to us, provided we don't get stuck in judgment and blame—so long as we don't try to hide the beach ball.

Judging by the abysmal failure rate of second and third marriages, it is obvious that one of the major reasons for divorce is that one or both did not let go emotionally and did not focus their intention on true healing. Only by resolving the old painful feelings will one be complete and able to move forward. When you choose to heal and let go, the door to discovering the self opens wide, and you get a heightened sense of self-awareness.

This translates into personal growth and deeper understanding. Becoming neutral or indifferent means you are no longer hooked into fighting and wasting precious energy. You have stopped getting into power struggles, and it is no longer important to prove that you are right or better than your ex.

In Tiam Dayton's dynamic book *Daily Affirmations for Forgiving and Moving On*, he writes,

> Letting go is an act of surrender, a recognition and acceptance of things as they are, a coming to grips with the fact we live in a less than perfect world. It is not just a thought but an actual cellular release, a constant daily process, a turning over.

Chapter 3

Grieving

Tools to Help You in Your Healing

The ending of a love relationship is a devastating experience. It hurts to be rejected and to have all your plans and dreams torn into a million pieces. It hurts to lose someone and to feel as though part of your life is gone.

When you have loved deeply, and the person is no longer with you, you miss him or her. This is normal. No matter how dysfunctional the relationship was, at one time, there were moments of happiness; dreams; and intimate times of laughing, touching, sharing, and caring. The painful reality is that your imagined future will not happen— at least not together. There are lots of lost dreams and hopes.

During the early stages of a breakup, it is easy to feel overwhelmed. It is easy to feel depressed and demotivated. You might wonder, *will this dark cloud ever lift? Will my mood and my initiative ever return to normal?* You have just experienced a major life event, one that affects many parts of your life.

When we are sad, mad, or anxious, we tend to be more sensitive than usual. We take things more personally. If someone doesn't return a call or text, we might find ourselves obsessing about why. It is easy to feel discouraged and wounded. If someone says something critical, even if it's meant to be helpful, we are left feeling devastated. Our ability to trust is often impacted, even our ability to trust ourselves. Thus, we postpone making decisions, getting out of our comfort zone, or trying new things. Many sleep a lot, eat a lot, drink a lot, or ruminate a lot. We might even second-guess ourselves. It's as though we go through a period when we do not trust ourselves. Our confidence has been shaken to the core. This dark period gives way to an opportunity to become introspective. Once we reach this level, there are endless growth possibilities. It does get better!

As with any relationship you have invested heavily in, the feeling of pain and loss needs to be resolved before you can move on. The process of grieving your lost relationship, which initially gave you love, joy, and hope, must take place before you can move forward into a new life. This grieving stage is essential when you separate from someone you once loved. It is a necessary part of coming to the other side and being healed. For this book, we will focus on healing from the death of a relationship. According to Ted Menten, author of *Gentle Closings: Facing Death and Saying Goodbye to Someone You Love,* "Some surveys indicate that as a nation, we have little or no patience with grieving people. Our society doesn't place a great deal of emphasis on the grieving process and we do not learn how to mourn our losses as it is not taught at our schools." So in the absence of knowing the rituals for grieving and mourning, we tend to cope with the pain, anxiety, and uncertainty of a lost relationship by looking for easy fixes and distractions. This sidestepping of the grieving process contributes to the divorce rate of more than 70 percent in second and third marriages.

It is necessary to work through the painful feelings to be healed and move on, for pain, if ignored, doesn't just disappear. At some point during our lifetime, we need to learn how to say goodbye. This skill is essential to dealing with any significant loss. Healing occurs best when we have the know-how, intention, and courage (*courage* comes from *coeur,* the French word for "heart") to work through the sad and painful feelings. We need to be willing to face loneliness, self-doubt, regret, and a plethora of difficult feelings to truly understand why our relationship has ended.

Grieving encompasses moving through the anger, sorrow, hurt, remorse, guilt, and conflict associated with letting go. Ultimately, we move toward acceptance and forgiveness—for both our ex and ourselves. This is what happens when we are complete. This allows us to successfully love again.

The grieving process is like going through a turbulent storm. At some point, the storm will be over, the sky will once again be sunny and blue, and if you look, you'll even get to experience a beautiful rainbow.

Grieving a lost relationship is an opportunity to become wiser, kinder, and more compassionate. It's an opportunity to heal with understanding while we forego blame or judgment. This can lead to excellent opportunities to know ourselves and take time to go within. The silence is a time for self-reflection, and we discover who we truly are and what our priorities are. It's important to know yourself before you embark on the next relationship. When you create a strong, positive relationship with yourself, you will indeed attract another who is on your emotional wavelength. Like attracts like; the law of attraction will prove this time and time again.

The more energy we put into a relationship, the longer the grieving process will take. Similarly, the deeper the cut, the longer the wound takes to heal. Imagine you've just undergone open-heart surgery. After that invasive and delicate surgery (what a shock to your system), you must follow the doctor's orders and be gentle with yourself as you slowly recover. By giving yourself the time you need to recover and not rushing, you will heal more deeply and more perfectly, which will enable you to get on with your life and enjoy every new moment.

During the healing process or convalescent period, you could slow down, learn to meditate, spend quality time with yourself, do your forgiveness work, and regroup. After all, you need to take the time to cry and grieve the death of the relationship. Yes, it takes courage to mourn and grieve, write your letters of completion, and resume your life. This is the perfect time for self-improvement. The payoff for this effort is tremendous. Having gone through a love relationship and its ending provides you with an opportunity to be healed and transformed. You are much better prepared for your new successful relationship. You have become clear about your values, and after reading this book, you will understand yourself and love yourself to a much greater degree. Remember, no one can ever take your self-esteem from you without your permission. No one can rob you of your self-love; that is your gift to yourself.

Embrace the grieving process. It is natural and healthy to cry. Crying doesn't mean you are weak; crying is a normal response to sadness. You need to feel your grief. Losses hurt; even welcome losses bring about pain and sadness. Dealing with heart-wrenching emotions is not easy, but if you set the intention to heal and move on with your life, you most assuredly will. Energy follows intention!

Grieving is a process that is ongoing. You need to cry and let out your sad feelings. Many begin crying and then find themselves sobbing. Sometimes a song may trigger tears, or it may be a movie, play, or book. Whatever your catalyst might be, know that tears are normal and necessary. You are releasing and expressing the sadness of an ending. You need to take little breaks to not feel overwhelmed by your sad and depressing emotions. Shower yourself with compassion, patience, and kindness during this most difficult time of your healing process. You also need to include healthy diversions as you go forward. While you are dealing with the pain of the grieving process, you are vulnerable and need the loving kindness of others to move through a myriad of difficult feelings. Many people try to sidestep or avoid this stage because it is so painful. To nurture yourself, you might consider taking a walk with a friend; going to a yoga or tai chi class; or getting a massage, facial, or reflexology. Consider enjoying a healthy meal with friends, going to a movie, or doing things you put off when you were in the relationship. These various options, these small breaks, will help you rejuvenate. You need to share your feelings. This will help in getting over your loss. Do not judge yourself. Use this transitional time to truly pamper and love yourself.

One exercise that is highly effective is a letting-go letter. By writing this letter, you will be taking an important step in healing and moving forward in your life. Write down the first thoughts that come to mind as you complete the letter.

A sample letter is as follows:

Dear _____,

I am sorry that _____
_____
_____

I feel sad about _____
_____

I will always remember _____
_____
_____

Thank you for _____

_____

_____

Goodbye.

_____

    Another exercise you might try that creates more introspection is measured breathing. This exercise is designed to open your heart, get you centered, and still your mind.

    First, find a comfortable position to sit in. Be still, close your eyes, clear your mind, and be present (be in the now). Next, take a deep breath in through your nose, and hold it. Wait a few moments, and then release the breath through your mouth. Release any tension your body might be holding. Repeat this breathing several times, making the exhalation longer than the inhalation each time. Trust your body, and let your body find itself. The body will release what it needs to release. Say the following to yourself:

- "I am breathing in; I am breathing out."
- "I am breathing in peace and breathing out sadness."
- "I am breathing in gratitude; I am breathing out pain."
- "Love is all there is. All is well."

Say these affirmations five to ten times before gently allowing your eyes to open while you bring yourself back to the room. Many find it helpful to count on their fingers. Many people use the breathing technique of going within to attain feelings of peace, hope, and love. They find the exercise to be effective. Take your time while doing this. Do not rush through it. Give yourself at least five minutes, and tailor the words so they will have meaning for you.

This next exercise will nourish your mind, body, and spirit. Begin by placing your hand over your heart. Say the following to your inner self:

- "I love you right here and right now. I love you exactly as you are. My love for you is pure; my love for you is eternal. I love you unconditionally; I love you right now and forever. I will always be here for you."
- "I will always take excellent care of you; you will get through this and be stronger and better off in the long run."
- "All is well, and I move forward one day and one moment at a time."

It is important that you focus on yourself and do self-care exercises every day. We are all different and all have different time tables regarding our healing time. We all grieve differently. For some, writing letter after letter of goodbye is effective, while others like to talk through their feelings. Some people turn to poetry, music, painting, sculpting, and writing stories. There is a great movie with Diane Keaton and Jack Nicholson called *Something's Gotta Give*, in which Diane Keaton uses writing to heal after her breakup. Some need to be still and turn within. The goal is to understand that we heal from the inside out.

Arthur Golden, in *Chicken Soup for the Soul*, puts it this way:

> Grief is a most peculiar thing. We're so helpless in the face of it. It's like a window that will simply open of its own accord. The room grows cold, and we can do nothing but shiver. But, it opens a little less each time, and a little less each day; and one day, we wonder what has become of it.

You can't start the next chapter of your life if you keep rereading the last one.
—Unknown

Finally is my figure-eight exercise. It's a great tool I've used over the years with my coaching clients that's highly effective in letting go, healing, and moving on. It goes like this:

1. First, begin by closing your eyes, breathing deeply, and visualizing the number 8 on its side.
2. Then visualize your ex-partner in the farthest loop of the infinite number 8. Place yourself at the other end.
3. As you tune in to your ex-partner, say the following (either to yourself or out loud):
   a. "I forgive you. I forgive me."
   b. "I am free. You are free."
   c. "I wish you love and peace. Love and peace come back to me."
   d. "I send you a blessing. Blessings come back to me."
   e. "Thank you, and goodbye."

Do as many rounds of this simple but powerful exercise as feels right to you. Many people find that by doing one or two at a time, they can feel a shift in energy. Some might do a double set one time only, while others might continue for several weeks. Most are in between. Trust your intuition to guide you to the proper level.

The famous metaphysical healer, author, and world-renowned speaker Louise Hay has stated, "What we give out comes back multiplied." This is something we all need to take in. The law of attraction will reinforce this concept as well. To heal and move on, it is vital to forgive your ex as well as yourself. Forgiveness occurs without judgment or blame. It is just another way of saying, "I choose to let go—with love, gratitude, and respect for what was." In this way, we wipe the slate clean and enjoy our new lives, living in the present moment with openness, gratitude, and inner peace.

Chapter 4

Releasing Blame

> Hatred is a banquet until you realize you are the main course.
>
> —Dr. Herbert Benson

Do you want to be bitter, or do you want to be better? Being stuck in the trap of bitterness will only rob you of your happiness as well as your inner peace. You cannot experience high self-esteem if you are living with blame, anger, or guilt.

When people choose *better*, they have arrived at a place where they want to grow and move beyond their self-doubts, forming a better relationship within themselves. This is the longest and greatest relationship you will ever have. Being able to understand and accept yourself is the first step in moving forward and growing emotionally.

Self-awareness is invaluable for being in a happy, healthy relationship.

Blame stunts growth and keeps us stuck in a rut that's extremely hard to get out of. The problem is that our ego constantly tells us we are right. If we're right, then the other person must be wrong. When we see the situation only from our lofty, self-righteous point of view, it becomes impossible to see the entire picture and learn from the agony of the breakup. A failed relationship carries a great deal of useful, life-altering, and transformative information. It creates the opportunity for us to become self-aware and, thus, empowered. When people refuse to look inward, they will, in time, find another partner to commit to, but the same lessons will keep reappearing. These lessons need to be identified and resolved, lest we go around and around, bouncing from relationship to relationship.

Many people stay stuck in blame. They happily point accusatory fingers at their partners and dredge up the hurts, disappointments, and injustices to avoid dealing with themselves and the painful feelings that come from their own shortcomings. The problem with pointing the finger is twofold. First, by blaming the other, you are putting yourself in the position of being a victim. This prevents you from seeing the part you played in the death of the relationship. Second, by keeping the anger alive, you sustain a strong negative energy. This energy binds two people together like a glue. I once heard a poem by an unknown author that sums up what happens in a relationship that keeps each partner stuck. It goes as follows:

> *Once to Embrace; Now to Abhor*
> *Ecstasy Past; Now Only War.*
> *Hatred's Our Bond, tourniquet tight.*
> *We cling closely together with all of*
> *our might.*

To stop acting like a victim or playing the victim role, we need to see how we participated in the demise of our relationship. This means we have an opportunity to learn and choose to be stronger and wiser.

We cannot blame external circumstances or people. You, and only you, are attracting certain people. Relationships are cocreated. It is imperative to know what your pattern is. Do you attract any of the following?

- Bad boys
- Needy women
- Addicts or people with addictions
- Emotionally unavailable men
- Manipulative women
- People who lie or cheat

- Angry men
- Workaholics
- Poor communicators
- People who are avoiders

Support yourself and congratulate yourself for having the courage to open your eyes and look at the pattern of your life. Being aware and consciously making choices are ways you can use your power. Being unconscious of your pattern is accepting your role as a victim. Until you learn to identify your pattern, it will continue to keep repeating, causing you the same heartache time after time.

Using the Word *Hurt*

By pointing a finger of blame at your ex and saying, "Look what you did to me," you are choosing the emotion of hurt. "I was the innocent victim of your horrible behavior."

This means you walk around with not only self-righteousness but also anger, resentment, hatred, and hurt. These emotions are not conducive to taking your power back. They are not conducive to healing and moving forward. It might be true that your former partner did not live up to the expectations you had in the relationship. Part of the process of facing the naked truth is that you need to be honest and open about *your* part in the relationship. Did you make yourself clear about what you expected and needed? Did you make your value system clear? Did you ignore red flags along the way? We are not always clear about our expectations. It often happens that people hint at what they expect and assume the other person recognizes how important their expectations are. Or perhaps you did express yourself, and your ex only gave lip service to your needs and values but did not live up to what was expected.

Take Mary Anne and Jim. During the two years that they dated, Mary Anne thought she was quite clear about family life being a top priority—not only her primary family, but she wanted to have a family of her own as well. Jim countered that with "I would only be comfortable with one child. I'm just not that into kids." Mary Anne accepted that strong statement from Jim, as she also loved her career as an interior designer. For six years, Mary Anne did not bring up the touchy subject of starting a family. Upon learning that her youngest sister was pregnant, Mary Anne sheepishly brought up the subject again. After all, she thought, now was a perfect time to discuss having children, as they were doing well financially. Jim had just received a promotion with a large bonus. Initially, the discussion did not go far. Jim wanted to talk about it in a year or so; he said he was much too stressed in his new position, and since it was such an important topic, they should revisit it when things settled down. Feeling at the end of her patience, Mary Anne made an appointment to see a marriage counselor. She blamed Jim for taking away her most fervent desire: having a child. She told him he was the cause of her autoimmune disease as well as her cluster migraines. She felt unfulfilled, unheard, and trivialized and was seething with resentments. She blamed him for denying her and causing her depression. The counselor helped them to uncover their deepest fears and express their feelings fully. Mary Anne and Jim learned how to communicate from the heart. They also learned how destructive blaming one another was. It nearly brought them to divorce.

After several years of counseling, they learned new effective tools of communication and focused their new energy on participating in the lives of their nieces and nephews who lived nearby. This bonding with the children brought Mary Anne and Jim much closer. They used their communication skills to develop greater intimacy with the children. When Jim's sister died unexpectedly, Jim's nephew, a twelve-year-old boy, was left orphaned. It was Jim who suggested Danny live with them, much to Mary Anne's delight. Mary Anne's dream of having a family had now become a reality. In retrospect, the universe had given them a trial run at parenting. Their time in therapy enabled them to improve their skills for bringing a family together. They had learned how valuable it was to openly express honesty and non-blaming communication and to take responsibility in conflict resolution.

Take Christie, a woman in her late forties, who was a successful entertainer. She was a beautiful, articulate, smart woman who had made lots of friends wherever she lived. She was also financially secure. She had experienced two toxic and draining divorces and wanted to work on issues pertaining to her current relationship of two years. She explained that this relationship was the one she was strongly committed to, as this was her true soulmate. They had much in common, were deeply in love, and wanted this special relationship to last forever. She went on to explain that she had given more to this relationship than she had ever given to any other relationship.

Christie prided herself on being a super-independent woman and found it difficult to admit to needing anyone. She stated that she was an alpha female, which rendered her incapable of being vulnerable in any relationship. She felt as though she always had to be in control. She admitted to never having said, "I'm sorry," or even having been the one to reach out to her partner after a spat or disagreement. She expected her partner to always come to her. As time went on, Christie came to understand that her behavior resulted in creating distance. Unbeknownst to her, she had put up huge walls. She also had several self-limiting beliefs that had gotten in the way: "I don't need anyone," "I'm totally strong and self-sufficient," and "It's dangerous and scary to let a man get too close." She believed that relationships are always painful. Of course, these self-limiting beliefs were created in childhood, but ultimately, they kept all the important men in her life at arm's length. After every breakup, Christie found a replacement quickly and told herself she was healed and ready, when

- she hadn't gone through a mourning or grieving period;
- she hadn't a clue as to what she had contributed to the failure of each relationship; and
- she lacked self-awareness, humility, and introspection.

Since she was a busy person, distractions were easy for Christie. Eventually, she focused on doing some inner work and getting in touch with her true self. She wanted to change her self-limiting beliefs around relationships, as these beliefs had been getting in her way. By getting in touch with her emotions and her needs, she began to develop an understanding as well as an acceptance of who she was on the inside. She learned to trust and be vulnerable for the first time.

Her partner also opted to do some inner work, wanting to strengthen their relationship and do some growing of his own. He was open, nurturing, loving, and caring. They deepened their relationship by sharing their fears, insecurities, and hopes with one another. Eventually, both were able to cry together during times of deep sharing. They learned that many of their own fears were mirrored in one another. In time, this couple created a truly intimate, healthy, fun, and fulfilling relationship that benefited both. They often referred to their partnership as a friendship that was precious—a treasured relationship between two people who bring out the best in each other. They learned invaluable communication tools. Together they turned a shallow relationship into one that had closeness and depth. They both made this prized relationship their number-one priority.

When we find ourselves locked in a blaming position, we prevent ourselves from having the benefits of emotional growth. We cannot see the role we played in the death of the relationship. It's all too easy to say, "He cheated on me!" However, it is necessary to be totally emotionally honest and say, "Our relationship had grown distant and stale. I knew deep down inside that something was definitely wrong." This will result in lifting the thick curtain of self-deception and denial. It takes a willingness to be emotionally open and requires us to pull the curtain back. We need to do some individual soul searching, and yes, it does take two to build complete honesty, trust, and closeness. If one partner drops the lines of communication, it is up to the other partner to pick them up. If your partner is your best friend, it is vital that you each make the relationship a priority. To keep your five-star status as a best friend, you must reassure each other that the goal of your relationship is to provide a safe, loving place for growth, security, and nurturance. The work and commitment put into developing a happy relationship will all be worth it!

Robin and Rick went through a bitter divorce. They had an eight-year-old daughter, Beth, at the time. Each partner wanted validation that he or she was the wronged party, so they would share intimate details of their marital discord with Beth ad infinitum. Poor Beth felt as if she were in the middle of a no-win war as each parent incessantly complained about his or her former partner to this innocent child. Beth would repeatedly ask them to stop, but her requests were ignored. She just wanted to feel free to love and adore each of her parents. She was not interested in who had done what to whom. When Beth was twelve, she developed an eating disorder that grew worse with each passing year. She tried running away from home. She tried overdosing on Mom's pills. In many unconscious ways, Beth was screaming, "Stop!" Robin and Rick called one another unfit parents. They fought for years over custody of their daughter, trying to cut each other out of Beth's life. Eventually, after numerous court appearances and expensive psychological tests, Beth was directed to live with her maternal grandparents. This was an arrangement she felt would offer freedom from the never-ending battle between her parents. Ultimately, each one of her parents faced health challenges, and Beth, for her own survival, relocated to another state to go to college. She married at age twenty, hoping to write a new chapter and fully disconnect from years of bitterness, hostility, and blame. For Beth, this had been a war that was ugly, painful, and endless.

Contrary to popular belief, the opposite of love is not hate; it is indifference. Indifference is the state when there is no longer a charge from your former partner. The connection has been broken. It is over. It is dead. To aspire to this level of indifference brings freedom. When we make this choice, it means that both people are now neutral toward one another. We are free, and our partners are free.

The former partner is no longer a person we give any energy to. We can fill our cup with new beneficial, positive energy and not use any emotional space for negative thoughts. Anger needs to be resolved lest we spend our energy focusing on a person from our past. This is like driving your car while constantly looking in the rearview mirror. We need to be completely present, living in the beauty and peace of the now. In this way, we open ourselves to the real healing and to our own personal growth.

Every adversity, every failure, every heartache carries with it the seed of an equal or greater benefit.

—Napoleon Hill

Chapter 5

Resolving Childhood Issues

What happened to us during our childhood has a huge impact on our adult relationships. At an unconscious level, we often repeat the same emotional dynamics we had with our siblings and parents. That primary relationship, that give and take, formed many basic patterns we carry with us into adulthood. We simply repeat those dynamics with our spouses, always gravitating toward the familiar and the predictable. The familiarity and blame keep us mired in the past like a hamster going around and around on a wheel. Self-awareness is the key that will unlock this unconscious pattern and thereby allow us to change and move to a new and better approach. We can then remove or alter our self-limiting beliefs.

Often, the abuse in a marriage reflects the abuse or neglect we received as children. Somehow, there's a familiar feeling that we are strangely comfortable with. We unconsciously choose the same type of partner who provides us with the predictability and familiarity of the past.

> Every person, all the events of your life are there because you have drawn them there. What you choose to do with them is up to you.
> —Richard Bach, *Illusions*

The abuse may or may not be overt. You might not have been your mother's favorite child. Perhaps you were born into a rocky, tempestuous marriage or were unplanned and got in the way of your mother's career. Maybe Mom did not have a lot of love to give because she never received it herself. Whatever the cause, it is common to marry someone who also makes you feel disrespected, worthless, and unlovable. This script, the old familiar feelings, get replayed over and over until a person is ready to look at the patterns being repeated, examine those motives, and make a conscious decision to change.

This cycle explains why there are so many people who find themselves having the same fights and issues with each new successive partner. This also explains why those who went through a divorce the first time have a greater likelihood that their second, third, or fourth marriage will also be unsuccessful.

Until we take the opportunity to heal our emotional wounds from childhood, we will continue to fail at our current relationships. It is imperative that we resolve the issues of the past. Every relationship provides the opportunity to address old issues that need to be resolved.

Brian grew up in a home in which all of the family members existed without closeness and intimacy. His was a family that did not connect with one another. For all intents and purposes, they could have been complete strangers living under one roof. For whatever reasons, the family members did not share their emotional selves. It wasn't until counseling that Brian learned he had been emotionally deprived as a child.

Brian's father, who was a successful business owner, spent little time engaging with his wife or with Brian, his only child. He spent every waking moment working on the business, and when the family went on vacation, he spent most of the day buried in paperwork. However, Brian's father was generous with his money and often told his wife that he worked as hard as he did so he could give her the best of everything. He would say, "I'm happy to work like a maniac so you can have a great life! You deserve a life of luxury."

Barbara S. Tucciarone, PsyD

Brian's mother habitually spent her days shopping, either alone or with her friends. She admitted to being a compulsive shopper and enjoyed the temporary high it gave her. She was constantly rearranging the decor and buying new additions to accommodate the change. She spent little time with Brian and shuttled him off to school at a young age.

Brian observed, while growing up, that two of his uncles fell on hard financial times and were eventually abandoned by their wives. The wives found wealthy replacements, and the uncles were left to fend for themselves. This experience was referenced several times at various family gatherings. This grew into a self-limiting belief for Brian that women were only interested in men who were successful and were great providers for them. He thought that if a man failed at that, he would lose his wife.

Growing up, Brian never saw or experienced closeness between his parents. They barely spent any time together, as Dad worked the business, and Mom did her compulsive shopping.

As an adult, Brian became involved with the family business. Like his father, he put in long days while his wife, Jessica, filled her emptiness with food and cooking. She went to cooking schools and would use cooking and baking as a way to numb her

54

feelings. However, after a medical scare when she'd just turned fifty, Jessica decided to change her life. She joined a gym and started exercising. She lost sixty pounds in a twelve-month period and became fitter and more self-confident. Simultaneously, she did some work on her self-esteem, developed more effective communication skills, and became more socially outgoing.

Not much later, Jessica announced that she was in love with another man and wanted a divorce. Shocked and blindsided, Brian pleaded and asked what the other man offered that he could not. What was it she needed? "Intimacy," she replied. She now felt understood, accepted, cherished, and close to someone for the first time. She explained that she felt Brian was absent from their relationship and did not care or share his feelings with her; their communication lacked any depth and closeness. She was thus drawn to this new man who wanted to be with her and enjoy her presence. Brian initially agonized over Jessica's decision to trade her secure life for a new one that offered closeness and greater intimacy. He felt overwhelmed and confused. He had provided security and wealth, as his father before him had, but it had proven to be his undoing. How could she want this?

His consternation led him to begin working on his own issues. Step one was to let go of an enormous amount of blame toward Jessica. Step two was to let go of the blame he had for himself. As time passed, Brian continued to work on releasing and resolving his angry, remorseful, and sad feelings. He realized he had been living in a shallow relationship for eighteen years. He came to understand that his marriage was a replica of his father and mother's marriage, which was a marriage between two polite strangers.

Many people find they repeat their childhood patterns. The selection of a partner is something that happens on an unconscious level. As we become more introspective, it is astonishing to discover that our partners have been pressing those sensitive wounds originating in childhood.

As Brian grew emotionally, he not only understood his relationship dynamics but also began to find out who he was and what he needed in a partner. He developed an authentic relationship with himself and realized that happiness was not tied to accumulating possessions and having wealth. Happiness was not on the outside but, rather, was attainable by changing the inside—his relationship with himself.

He eventually cut back his comfortable routine of hiding out at the office and made a commitment to create a healthy life balance. He began this new journey by making a list of what was most important to him. He discovered there were interests he had put on the back burner. He became aware that it was essential to have a healthy life, work, and play balance, and he continued to build his self-worth. Enjoying new interests, meditating, and cultivating supportive friendships became important. He was determined to enjoy new interests outside of the business. Brian used affirmations and changed his inner dialogue. He affirmed that he was getting ready for a healthy, fulfilling relationship with a person who was also emotionally available.

Brian realized he no longer needed to emulate his father by excessive work. Over time, he peeled back layers to find himself. Brian found happiness within as he became more and more self-confident and fulfilled. He began to truly enjoy his life for the first time. He could still hear Jessica's words when she'd announced that she was in love with someone else. She'd told him, "Someday you'll thank me for this. One day you'll see that I actually did you a favor." Well, that day had finally arrived.

In their popular book *Conscious Loving*, Drs. Gay and Kathleen Hendricks wrote,

> When we get close to another person, it brings to the surface our own unresolved issues from the past—the very things that you would least like to

look at. In adult life, the universe puts you in situation after situation allowing you the opportunity to embrace those things you have tried to hide and hide from the past.

Jennifer's father was a control freak. He would not confer with his wife over joint decisions and would often make commitments for his wife. He would say things like "I told them you'd be happy to serve on that committee." Additionally, he had a habit of checking up on his wife's tasks. He would wash the pots and pans after his wife had already cleaned them. He would restack the dishwasher, thinking that his way was the better way. It was common for him to run his finger over the mantel, checking for dust or grime spots that had been missed. He never missed an opportunity to announce his findings when he found a spot. Large decisions were his to make as well. He would announce that he had called a Realtor because it was time to move, and he had found a larger house or a better neighborhood.

His wife would nod in agreement and say, "All right." There was no discussion and no input from her. He made decisions for Jennifer and her brother, Bobby, as well. Bobby rebelled during adolescence and was often grounded and punished, while Jen meekly followed her mother's example and quietly went along with her father's choices. The small number of times when she tried to question him or disagree, she was quickly shut down, and he would say that the decision had been made and that she should appreciate his concern for her. Jen could still see her father looking at her with contempt. This often made her feel as if she should have pleased him and not even questioned his authority.

When Jen entered coaching, she stated that she needed to find her voice in her marriage. She had been told by her holistic physician that her IBS was related to stress. This statement had been a wake-up call for her. Her best friend also had suffered from IBS, and through changing her diet as well as her behavior, she had been symptom free for the last four years. She told Jen that through her coaching sessions, she had learned to speak up for herself and found effective ways to manage her stress. When Jen came to see me, I asked her what her three greatest wishes would be. Without hesitation, she responded that she wanted to improve her communication skills, be more confident, and find her voice. Initially, Jen and I worked on increasing her self-care. She began making choices that were self-nurturing and self-validating by being more organized and improving her diet, sleep, and exercise routines. As her personal successes multiplied, her motivational level skyrocketed. She learned that she deserved the exhilarating feeling of giving herself permission rather than seeking it from someone else. This permission included the right to say no. She came to realize that the most important person to please was herself.

Eventually, Jen's wish of finding her voice was fulfilled. She learned to use her new voice—initially with her friends, then with her colleagues at work, and ultimately with her husband. Interestingly, Jen had chosen to marry a man like her father. He loved making unilateral decisions and being in charge. Mark, her husband, began his own therapy to deal with a painful and sudden loss in his life. Unexpectedly, his father, who was also his best friend, had been killed. Mark wanted to get help for the big hole this loss had left in him. About that time, Jen entered life coaching. In his therapy, Mark came to realize that the only person he could control was himself. For the first time, Mark learned how to be introspective and find out what his needs, wants, and desires were. He learned how to get in touch with and express his feelings, which served him well in the resolution of his father's premature death. Both partners learned how to fully love and respect themselves as they took their respective journeys within. This couple learned to communicate more effectively and began to employ a technique called active listening as they spoke from their hearts to one another. They became good at resolving issues while negotiating with one another. By learning how to be vulnerable, they created a strong connection between them. They learned how to be vulnerable and began enjoying a level of true intimacy for the first time.

It has been some time since I have been in therapy; still, I can vividly recall my therapist saying to me, "Marriage forces us to deal with childhood core issues—the issues that are left over from our early development." Yes, it's often true that a partner pushes our buttons. It helps to remember that these buttons were installed long before we entered our relationship.

Chapter 6

Living with Yourself

What Is It like to Live with You on a Bad Day?

The ending of a relationship provides a wonderful opportunity for personal growth. Questions we need to ask ourselves include "What am I like when I don't get my way?" and "What's it like to live with me?" It is likely we will be subjective in our response to this question unless we are extremely self-aware. We could ask a former lover or long-term friend this question, provided he or she is caring, articulate, nonjudgmental, and observant.

Nicole asked Josh this question after they broke up. They had lived together for six years and knew each other well. She trusted Josh to paint a full picture. Of course, what he told her was from his perspective. First, Josh pointed out many positive qualities. He told her she was good-hearted, caring, warm, thoughtful, generous, flexible, compassionate, and bright. He appreciated the fact that she was neat, organized, practical, success-oriented, and hardworking. He also told Nicole that he felt she had some anger issues. He explained that it seemed to him that she took too many things personally. Also, she would scream and lose it and then talk about it only from her point of view for several days afterward. He admitted to being fearful of her explosive, volcanic episodes. He had distanced from her by spending more and more time helping others and working longer hours. Nicole thanked him for being kind when he shared this information with her. They had parted about eighteen months before under amicable circumstances. Together they'd realized they had different values as well as conflicting goals and would be better off parting.

We can turn our focus outward and be clear about what was wrong with our partner. This is commonplace. When we focus outward, we deprive ourselves of the chance to grow, turn inward, and understand ourselves more intimately. Knowing ourselves and loving ourselves unconditionally truly the way we are is having the perfect relationship. When we choose to stop pointing that finger of blame outward and focus, without judgment or blame, on what our part was in the ending of the relationship, we are on a better path. We will be able to attain self-acceptance, self-growth, and self-love. It takes courage to be emotionally naked with ourselves. We need to see who we are and what our needs in a relationship are.

Do Any of These Behaviors Ring True?

~The Immature Adult or the Under-Responsible~

Under-responsible people in a relationship are constantly trying to see what they can get away with. They are challenged by just how far they can push the envelope. There is an expectancy that someone else will always clean up their messes. They are like perpetual adolescents, having an unstoppable need to rebel—against promises, rules, laws, agreements, etc.

These people have difficulty getting along with others, which often manifests at their jobs or when working for someone else. They do not like to be told what to do. The immature thinking of the under-responsible partner is *I'll worry about that later.* These individuals are often late for appointments and late with financial payments, get into financial trouble, and wind up borrowing from others. They cope by putting their heads in the sand, ignoring their obligations, and ignoring the needs of others.

They often wind up with partners who are overly responsible.

Tommy moved from job to job during the thirteen years he was married to Maureen. During the downtime between positions, this couple used credit cards to pay for their living expenses. They were barely able to keep their heads above water. Maureen would take temp jobs to keep things going. It was especially stressful for her, as she had two young children. In time, Maureen was hired for full-time work. She moved up the professional ladder rapidly. The more success Maureen had, the more Tommy would slack off. Ultimately, Maureen asked Tommy to take over the household chores while she committed herself to her job. Tommy did not make dinner but, rather, took the kids out for fast food night after night. He often tossed them into bed without their bedtime rituals and barely maintained the house. The house was turned upside down day after day, week after week. Clearly, Tommy was refusing to carry his responsibilities as a husband and father. He became addicted to watching old movies on TV, surfing the Internet, and playing games. Maureen did some introspection and realized she had three kids to take care of. She also realized she was programmed to be overly responsible and therefore had partnered up with someone who was under-responsible. She often said that her marriage reminded her of the movie *Mrs. Doubtfire*.

Initially, Maureen felt that 100 percent of the problems in the marriage were directly related to Tom's immaturity. She came to see that she had a need to be a caretaker at an unconscious level and had found a partner to take care of. Her self-awareness became the catalyst to change her old script. It was freeing and empowering for Maureen to understand where she had been out of balance. Thus, she was now inspired to do the inner work of nurturing herself and creating a more balanced life.

~Relationship Addicts~

Relationship addicts are obsessed with being in a relationship. They are miserable when they are alone and hate to be with themselves. Since they believe they must have a partner, they jump from one relationship to another; any warm body will do. Usually, these people have another person being warmed up in the bullpen the minute their current relationship develops a wrinkle. In this way, they protect themselves from being alone.

When they focus on their partner, they can avoid focusing on themselves and never succeed in healing their lack of self-love. The other person serves as a distraction and prevents them from doing the work necessary to grow and be self-aware.

The two vital ingredients necessary for a healthy relationship are self-esteem and self-respect. Codependents or relationship addicts lack these qualities and thus become incredibly needy. They often complain that their partner does not give them the intimacy, time, or attention they need. Enough is never enough! Thus, their complaint is that they never get the sense of self-assurance necessary to grow and mature in their relationship. Emotionally, they are stuck, and they repeatedly move on to another relationship to try to capture the love they so desperately need.

~The Passive Aggressive~

These people usually act like nice, sweet people. They find it hard to say no because they are looking for approval outside of themselves. They cause harm or inconvenience unconsciously. They make others more important than themselves, which causes them to harbor a great deal of unconscious anger. This is subconscious anger—anger they are not even aware of. Thus, this anger is discharged in subversive ways. One could say they act out their anger quietly.

For example, when the kids were out on a daylong hike, John painted the family room but did not put up a sign warning anyone that the paint was wet. When the kids came back home, all three got white paint on their clothes and complained. John said, "Oh, sorry. I meant to put up a sign, but I must have forgotten."

Sharon received a recipe from Susan and made the meal for her boss and his wife. It tasted horrible and embarrassed her so much that she had to send out for Chinese. The next day, when she confronted Susan, Susan said, "I meant to tell you to exclude the cream, double the butter, and bake it for twenty minutes more. Sorry!"

Showing up late not once but almost all the time is another telltale sign of a passive-aggressive personality. "Yes, I know we'll be late for the show, but I misplaced my keys, and then I had to change my jacket. It took me awhile to find a better one. I feel bad about making you wait so long. Perhaps if we drive fast and hit all green lights, we can make it by intermission. I couldn't call you because my cell phone was out of juice. Sorry!"

Danielle shows up at your dinner without the dessert she promised to make. "Oh, sorry. I completely forgot I was supposed to make the pies. You should have called me to remind me!"

In the passive-aggressive personality, there is a great deal of "forgetting." The list of forgotten items, promises, and broken trust goes on and on. There is a myriad of ways this personality withholds. There is always an inconvenience to others, which the passive-aggressive persons try to cover up with an apology. Passive-aggressive people are quietly angry and act out that anger in subtle, manipulative, unconscious ways.

~The Stubborn~

Stubborn people are rigid and do not use the option of compromising in situations that require negotiation. They are opinionated, inflexible, and not good at listening, which is an invaluable skill necessary for creating a happy relationship. Ultimately, they push people away, as they are true loners. Stubbornness stems from an underlying personality problem that is fueled by inadequacy and anxiety. These people would rather fight to be right than resolve issues. Compromise is necessary to attain conflict resolution, as acceptance and respect are key ingredients for a relationship to succeed.

In their coaching, Carol and Sal presented with a problem concerning lack of sexual activity in their relationship. They had been married for nine years and had not had sexual relations in more than five years. They had a well-developed brother-sister relationship in that they hiked together, played tennis together, and shared many church-related activities together. However, after dinner, they went to their separate bedrooms on opposite sides of the house. Carol had been using the pill for birth control since she was in her teens. She announced to Sal that she wanted him to start using condoms. "After all," she said, "I have been responsible for birth control all this time; now it's your turn."

When Sal heard this, he said, "No way. I haven't used condoms in forever, and I know they ruin the feeling." Carol respond, "Then we won't have sex!" Of course, this couple realized they could have considered a vasectomy, tubal ligation, or other options, but they had both dug their heels in, and they refused to consider any other option. It is not uncommon for stubborn couples to enter power struggles. Power struggles distract from facing the emptiness of the relationship—the lack of emotional intimacy. In this situation, both individuals had secret lives they were unwilling to share with one another. After considerable exploration of needs and options, this couple decided to go their separate ways, refusing to negotiate or compromise. They jointly agreed, each to him- or herself, that they were right and their partner was wrong.

Joel and Michelle had been seeing one another for three years. During that time, Michelle made it clear she had a passion for travel. She worked long hours as a business owner and lived for the trips to faraway places. During the first two years of their relationship, Joel went through the motions of being satisfied with taking annual vacations. He often hinted that they should do other things with their money aside from traveling. Joel had a high-paying professional position, so money was not an issue. During the third year, Joel suggested they relax at his McMansion and take day trips; Michelle refused and said she wanted to travel. She proposed that they take a one-week cruise and *then* follow his suggestion. Refusing her compromise, Joel argued that he had a beautiful home, and there was no reason they shouldn't just kick back and enjoy it. She thought about this for a time and then proposed that she take a one-week cruise with one of her girlfriends and *then* spend the second week at his house. This angered Joel. His stubbornness just grew and grew. He ultimately told her she could do whatever she wanted, but the relationship was over. Michelle cruised for one week, and when she returned, Joel refused any contact with her. He would not come to her house to retrieve his belongings or give her back her key. There was radio silence. He had made up his mind that he was right, and she was wrong. There was no further discussion, just a complete and total cutoff. Joel had taken a rigid position, as is often the case with stubborn people. They display a "My way or the highway!" type of thinking. This inflexibility is destructive to closeness, trust, caring, and conflict resolution in a couple ship.

~The Pleaser~

The pleaser could also be called a codependent, as the pleaser will always put everyone else first.

Pleasers believe that everyone else's needs, opinions, and feelings are more important than their own. They believe that by submerging their needs and placing others in the number-one position, they will be liked. This behavior most often stems from childhood. The pleaser became overly focused on Mom and Dad getting their needs met. Then, during adolescence, the teen was not able to individuate. Individuating is a normal and healthy aspect of adolescence. Teens need to explore, experiment, and find out who they are and what they like and dislike as they attempt to develop an identity. The result of failure to individuate is adults who are uncertain of what they want out of life and who they are. They live to please others. Additionally, they do not truly like themselves. In most cases, they avoid taking emotional risks and look to take the easy and safe route. It is difficult for them to express themselves.

Stephanie grew up as the eldest of five children. She remembers constantly helping Mom with the other kids, meals, and laundry. She learned the art of pleasing at a young age, sacrificing her needs for the needs of the family. She also walked on eggshells around her mother, who suffered from severe depression and had fits of screaming rage. As an attempt to please her mother, Stephanie chose nursing as a career. She'd heard repeatedly that her mom had wanted to be a nurse but instead found herself pregnant, which had resulted in an early marriage.

At the age of twenty-three, Stephanie met a man with whom she fell in love. Eric asked Stephanie to marry him and told her how much it would mean if they married in a Presbyterian church. Stephanie quickly agreed, even though she was a devout Catholic. This was the first of many concessions she made to keep the peace. About ten years into the marriage, Eric suggested that his widowed mother move in with them. She was a critical, rigid, and overbearing woman. Again, Stephanie acquiesced, knowing that this woman would ultimately dictate how the house would be run and would ride roughshod over her.

Stephanie went back to work to avoid the critical nature of her mother-in-law. As time went on, Stephanie became more and more depressed and complained about being tired all the time. Eventually, she was diagnosed with two autoimmune diseases.

A neighbor suggested she see a counselor who could help with the low energy and the depression. This was a turning point for her. She began to see how, in trying to please others, she had lost herself. After a year, she felt like a new woman. She had become her own person by learning to love herself for the first time. Eric joined her in counseling, and in time, the couple worked on their relationship and became stronger together.

One by-product of pleasers is that they carry an enormous amount of repressed anger, also known as resentment, which is dangerous to one's emotional and physical health.

~The Constant Critic~

These people are perfectionists. Since there is no such thing as perfection, others are always falling short of impossible expectations. All others around them fall short as well. They point a finger of blame and judgment at their partner so they can temporarily distract from dealing with their own inner frustrations and low self-esteem. The partners who are involved with constant critics receive little praise but lots of judgments and complaints. Furthermore, every flaw and mistake is pointed out to them, which makes them feel put down and diminished. Living with a constant critic is difficult. Partners often clam up and stop sharing their experiences, feelings, and opinions. They stop feeling safe and are frequently on guard, anticipating the next complaint.

Constant critics are quick to say things like "Well, it took you long enough," "That's the most ridiculous thing I've ever heard; you've got to be kidding," and "What in the world were you thinking?" Constant critics often use sarcasm. Sarcasm is another form of criticism.

The critics play the role of the know-it-all, acting condescending toward others, their partners included. Thus, partners feel on guard and do not feel safe. They often edit what they say, preventing the relationship from developing depth. Often, their partners will find ways to numb out, a form of escapism. They distance from the critic by hiding out at work, being super busy, overeating, having affairs, and the like. Eventually, the partners become overloaded with frustrations and resentments and might walk away from the relationship.

Criticizing is another way to shift the focus from oneself onto another, thereby shifting and causing a distraction. Criticism is anathema to trust, happiness, and intimacy in a relationship. By focusing on another, the critic does not have to face the fact that he or she is intolerant, condescending, and incapable of loving. Critics escape from having a loving relationship with themselves.

~Romance Addicts~

Romance addicts are looking for the *perfect* mate. They love the idea of a relationship—any relationship. They are all about moonlight, violins, and roses. They are in love with love, as the saying goes. They are good at covering up the fact that they are not good with true intimacy. They do not know how to develop a supportive and deep friendship with another. Furthermore, they do not understand how to be vulnerable, which is necessary to create emotional intimacy. By squirting a lot of whipped cream on the outside, so to speak, they successfully cover up the fact that they are lacking on the inside. These people will sing romantic love songs, write beautiful romantic poems, give lavish gifts, and the like as they bend over backward to create a dazzling and impressive Hollywood atmosphere. All this is done to create the illusion of romance and lots of glitter. The glitter is good at covering up their shallowness. This prevents them from enjoying intimate relationships. Often, they have secrets. They lack the ability to be vulnerable and speak from the heart.

Romance addicts idolize their partner, placing him or her on a pedestal. They have illusions about their partner and never recognize who their partner truly is. Their fantasies provide them with a high much like a shopaholic gets from making purchase after purchase. They fail to understand that happiness comes from within. They believe pleasure equates to happiness, using their good looks, generosity, and charm to regale the object of their affection. They live in a fantasy world, as romantic love is based on illusion.

Fantasies don't last, and romantic love dies. In an authentic relationship, each person knows, understands, and accepts the other's strengths and weaknesses. That is what is known as unconditional love.

~The Self-Absorbed~

The self-absorbed are consumed with both looking good and feeling good; it's all about them. Bragging and showing off are daily occurrences for the self-absorbed.

When Mike and Marie met at work, Marie was impressed with Mike's cavalier, can-do attitude. He enjoyed living on the edge and regaled her with stories of the daring adventures and risks he had taken. He spoke of his bigger-than-life goals with enthusiasm and conviction. She was overwhelmed, and soon they were married.

After being married for twelve years, Michael began growing bored with his marriage; this included his magnificent home, his large boat, the country club membership, and his unbelievable jewelry and gun collection. Having just turned fifty, he decided it was time to change things. Michael began these changes by losing weight, going to a tanning salon, and working out with extreme fervor at a fancy gym. He developed an entirely new body with a new hairstyle to match. Much to his wife's surprise, he started taking steroids to aid in his body mass. He said he wanted to look better than all his professional competitors.

After announcing to his wife that he needed space (to be with a younger woman), he walked out on his family to live on his yacht. As if this were not bad enough, he liquidated all his investments, explaining that he needed the money to pay back other family members who had loaned him money. He also lied and said that they were in tremendous debt and that much of the money was to pay back creditors. "And what about us?" Marie asked. His answer was that she should sell the house, live in an apartment, and think about finding a job. He said he no longer wanted to be married, and she should figure out how to be more independent. Shortly thereafter, Mike and his girlfriend traveled to exotic places, taking one luxury vacation after another.

Marie found a wonderful therapist to work with. Initially, she needed to deal with the shock and heartbreak brought on by Mike's abandonment and rejection. It was as though her entire world had changed in an instant. When she entered counseling, she felt unworthy, unlovable, and frightened.

Marie came to discover that her crisis wasn't about a man going through a midlife crisis; rather, the marriage had been out of balance for years. She was a compulsive giver. She delighted in making him happy and pleasing him. On the other hand, Mike was a taker. He did not reciprocate her kindness, thoughtfulness, or generosity. However, Marie permitted it to be that way.

During Marie's counseling, she discovered that she had been neglected and abused in her childhood. She began to see that she'd accepted crumbs for years because that was her comfort zone. Additionally, once Marie saw that Mike was her dynamic opposite, it gave her the opportunity to learn the life lesson of being true to your passions and speaking your truth. In time, Marie found her voice and realized she had value as a person. Marie learned she was worthy. She began to practice a life-changing self-care routine as she took her power back. She learned to identify and experience her many passions and use her assertiveness skills. She developed an aspect of her personality that had been dormant. She learned that she did not need Mike to make her happy, nor did she need constant drama. Marie developed her identity and became a dynamic woman in her own right.

By using her previous work experience, intelligence, and high level of motivation, Marie wound up getting hired by a Fortune 500 company that greatly appreciated her. In a short time, Marie was promoted to a fulfilling position that paid well and made good use of her many talents.

Marie felt she had transformed because of this painful and devastating ordeal. She liked to say, "From bad comes good." Along with developing a sense of self-worth, Marie set her own goals as she continued to put self-care at the top of her priority list.

Mike, on the other hand, continued his self-absorbed pattern. He defied several court orders, refusing to be financially responsible for his two young sons. He fraudulently used the joint divorce settlement money and wound up in jail. In this case, a man went from being self-absorbed to self-destructive.

Chapter 7

Gifts from the Relationship

> A relationship is more of an assignment
> than a choice. We can walk away from the
> assignment, but we cannot walk away from
> the lessons it presents. We stay with a
> relationship until a lesson is learned, or we
> simply learn it another way.
> —Marianne Williamson

Every person we attract into our lives is there to help propel us forward on our life's journey. For starters, he or she brings to the surface parts of ourselves that need to be healed, parts of ourselves that we keep hidden. (See chapter 5, "Resolving Childhood Issues.")

The people who come into our lives are either lovers or teachers; sometimes they are both. The lovers may be family members, colleagues, friends, or neighbors. They are there for us through thick and thin; they help us to be better people. They have come into our lives to support us. They love us unconditionally. The teachers are those who have caused us pain.

Whatever the relationship, the resulting support is easy to understand when we create bonds of a fulfilling, nourishing friendship with another and when we meet people who love us in return.

We can all relate to people who are kind, loving, and adoring. We hope these treasured people will stay in our lives forever. We think of them as angels who help us to trust and let love in. We pray for them as we lay our heads on our pillow.

People who have hurt us, disappointed us, and even betrayed us can be our greatest teachers. We can choose to reject them, wanting revenge and retaliation, or we can learn from our experiences with them. As part of the learning process, I teach my clients the technique of reframing and introduce them to the mirroring concept. In reframing, thoughts are changed to empower us and make us feel better about an event or ourselves.

We can say, "He dumped me!" and feel angry and deceived, or we can tell ourselves the truth: "The relationship wasn't making either one of us truly happy and fulfilled. He simply initiated the split before I did."

Reframing is how we interpret our experiences and alter the perception of our own lives. We can choose to interpret what happens to us either in a demeaning way or in a life-affirming way.

In another case, my client Mary stated, "John felt I was unattractive and overweight, so he started having an affair with this so-called blonde bombshell at work. He claimed to be madly in love with her. I guess she's got the body and youth I don't have." After some work, Mary chose to reframe her situation as "John and I broke up. We both wanted different things out of life. We even had different values. I am now choosing to process my feelings, focus my energy on healing, and move forward. I intend to get to know myself better, and eventually, I will be in a partnership with a man who will meet my needs."

The mirroring concept provides a reflection of external feedback and is another valuable tool for personal growth. The situations in our lives can help us to know ourselves better. Shakti Gawain, best-selling author and workshop leader, explains, "The external world is like a giant mirror which reflects both our spirits and our forms clearly and accurately. Once we learn how to consider it and perceive and interpret its reflection, we have a fabulous tool." For example, if you realize your former partner broke promises to you, examine the relationship you have with yourself. Where in your life are *you* breaking promises to yourself? Another example might be with cheating or lying. If this behavior is something that existed in your previous relationship, take a long and honest look at your life, and ask yourself, "Where and how do I cheat or lie?"

The external also mirrors back our internal world in the area of being critical and judgmental. When we step back and are willing to take an open and honest look at ourselves, we will discover that the critical person is mirroring something back to us. This now becomes a gift; it empowers us with precious insights. People treat us the way we treat ourselves.

We have many opportunities to grow and be much happier within ourselves as we continue to release and heal aspects of our own internal relationship. This mirroring aspect provides external feedback that helps us to see ourselves, without judgment, at a deeper level. Therefore, we are more open and receptive to learning the lessons presented. As Shakti Gawain goes on to state in her book *Living in the Light,* "Whatever comes into our lives and transforms us is to be celebrated."

In my own life, I had been a people pleaser. One aspect of my focusing outwardly and wanting others to be happy was that I neglected to set boundaries. I came to realize this through my own time in counseling. I had ignored my own needs while being overly focused on others' needs. After complaining to my therapist that I felt little or no respect from those who were most important to me, I was introduced to the mirroring concept. I spent the next several days meditating on the question "Where and how do I fail to show respect to myself?" I realized the people in my life were simply mirroring back the relationship I had with myself. If people were disrespectful to me, it was because I was disrespectful to myself. Realizing this, I began the work to change the relationship I had with myself. Throughout the years, I have shared with my clients the fact that if **you** change, the people around you will change as well. They will mirror the new you.

Best-selling author and workshop leader Debbie Ford states, "There are no accidents. To complete the process of taking responsibility we must acknowledge that, at some level, for some reason, we attracted our partner into our lives."

The law of attraction teaches us that whatever we give out returns to us. It is like a mirror. If we are happy or send out positive vibrations, then we will see positive vibrations returning. When they return, you will notice them in situations and people showing up in your life in a positive way.

Basically, we need to be open and receptive to the concept that we attract the people who help us to grow emotionally. There are parts of ourselves that we are not aware of; those parts are hidden from us. They exist at a deep subconscious level.

Take Erica and Pete. Erica was a logical, cerebral, quiet person. She had been raised in a household in which the family members suppressed their anger. Mom and Dad never raised their voices. It was pointed out to Erica and her siblings that intelligent, educated people will always put themselves in other people's shoes to try to understand where they might be coming from. They were also programmed with the idea that it was far better to discuss a conflict later, when the emotional climate was calm. Erica's way of handling her emotions was to think about them first, attempt to understand them, and use logic. She went out of her way to avoid any type of confrontation. Pete, on the other hand, would yell and slam doors, blowing off emotional steam whenever he was upset. Everyone knew when Pete was angry. Pete would announce, "I'm so frustrated. I'll be back from my run in a half hour!"

During their marriage, Erica would tell Pete that his outbursts of anger were savage and uncalled for. She eventually admitted that she was frightened by his outbursts and hated it when Pete raised his voice.

During coaching sessions, she learned that her fear masked her own underlying anger. This anger, at her parents, had been festering beneath the surface. When Erica finally understood that she had been carrying this unresolved anger deep within herself, she identified one of the gifts Pete brought to the relationship. By uncovering this gift, Erica focused on the opportunity to resolve her anger. In this way, her partner showed her parts of herself that lay hidden. As Debbie Ford teaches,

> I am your mirror and you are mine. We were created with the reflective device of being able to see ourselves in each other. I can see myself every time I look at you. The outer world is my mirror, and when I see your kindness I can view my own kindness. If I look at you and see your greed, I am seeing my own greed. If I look at you and see your generosity I am seeing my own.

Going back to my own story, one day as I sat in silence, the answer came quickly to the surface. My pattern was that I let people take advantage of me and did not object. I had turned my anger inward, causing myself to suffer from severe headaches. Suddenly, my pattern became crystal clear. Happy to understand this, I began to say no when I felt the need and set boundaries for others, telling them what I wanted. I told myself that my needs were my responsibility, and I realized that it was up to me to communicate by being direct and authentic. I was willing to focus on self-fulfillment and love. People whom I had once permitted to make demands on my life and drain my energy and to whom I dedicated time were now being told no on occasion. When I began respecting myself, the people who took advantage of me began to change and treated me differently. I changed the rules of the game, and they began to treat me with the respect and kindness I deserved. I was now a believer.

During the years since my understanding, I have learned to pay attention to the invaluable lessons that clients, friends, family, and even strangers are teaching me. I remember a quote from Arthur Rubinstein that said, "I have found that if you love life, life will love you right back."

To love truly, you must first love yourself. If you are critical of your shortcomings, you will be critical of the shortcomings of others. If you are impatient with yourself, you will be impatient with others. Similarly, if you are judgmental of yourself, you will be judgmental of others. You will also attract judgmental people into your life who are mirrors of you. It is important to make self-love a priority, as when all is peaceful, loving, and joyful on the inside, the outside will reflect that as well.

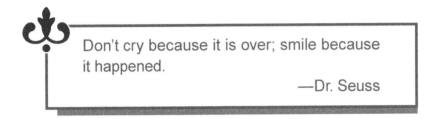

> Don't cry because it is over; smile because it happened.
>
> —Dr. Seuss

Everything we experience has value. Everything teaches us. Every experience is designed to enrich us and make us more self-aware. When we choose to be open-minded and optimistic, we can step back and ask ourselves what the golden nuggets we received from the relationship were.

We benefit greatly when we choose to focus on the gifts we received from our former relationship. There existed an energy exchange that had value for both; for a segment in time, two people shared a journey together. Now that journey has come to an end. If we are emotionally honest, we will be able to see many things the relationship provided for us. After all, we are wiser, more experienced, and even more evolved than when we first entered the relationship. Choosing to express appreciation and gratitude for the gifts from a painful, disappointing experience improves our sense of self-esteem and our physical health; it catapults us to our next level of emotional growth.

If we deliberately choose to embrace the change and not push back against it, we will choose to be better and not bitter.

Here's an exercise for practice. Take out a pad of paper and list the gifts you received in your past relationships. As a guide, here are some examples:

- She showed me how to be vulnerable. I never knew I could cry.
- He accepted me even though I had a double mastectomy. I was so self-conscious. I never knew that my body was still sexy and that I could still be desired.
- I know that my religion matters a great deal to me. This is an important value, and I will honor it next time.
- I never knew I could fall in love so deeply and passionately.
- He introduced me to the world of investing and money. I learned to understand and appreciate money and planning.
- She introduced me to the world of travel. This opened my horizons.

- She showed me that I had emotional needs. I've always been so logical and bottled up. I will always be grateful.
- He showed me that sex could be fun.
- He introduced me to golf.
- She taught me how to dress and improve my looks.
- She helped me repair my relationship with my kids.
- She taught me much better communication skills.
- He introduced me to eating well and making good nutritional choices. Largely because of him, I recovered from Lyme disease.
- I no longer have issues with insomnia. She taught me to stick to a regular bedtime schedule and relax.
- He taught me to respect my body and treat myself well; I will continue to get my weekly massage because of him.
- I can ski! She taught me the beauty of it and introduced me to a whole new world.
- Because of Laura and the interior decorating skills I learned from her, my house is now a home and looks beautiful.
- He showed me the difference between religion and spirituality. I now meditate daily, and I am so much more at peace now.

- I bought my first convertible thanks to Beth. I love it!
- Nicole was an awesome support during my mom's prolonged illness and eventual death. I will always be grateful for her patience, devotion, and kindness.
- Chris was there for me through my illness and the death of my precious little dog. It was the most traumatic experience ever. I will always be grateful for his kindness, love, and support.
- Thanks to David, I now adore symphonies, opera, and music. I have many memories of the great moments we enjoyed together.

As seasons change, so do relationships. Having spent time with another person, having learned much, and having been transformed, we are now becoming ready for the next stage of our personal growth.

Live in the present.
Embrace every event without
judgment or blame.

Chapter 8

Forgiveness

> Forgiveness wipes the slate clean so you can allow other better things to come in.
> —Louise Hay

Forgiveness tends to be a challenge for many folks. Consider the following statements:

- "Why should I forgive someone who betrayed me? After all, I was the injured party!"
- "He wanted out. I was willing to work on our relationship, and he wanted to end it! Why should I forgive him, when he's the one who caused so much pain?"
- "Why should I forgive someone who doesn't deserve to be forgiven?"

If any of these thoughts sound familiar, read on.

First, forgiveness does not mean to sanction or pardon. Forgiveness does not mean what the other person did was acceptable. Forgiveness means that we make a conscious choice to let go of yesterday. We do not make this choice for the other person. We make this choice for ourselves. The other person is still accountable for his or her behavior.

When we choose to forgive, we stop playing the role of the blamer; we stop playing the role of the victim; and most importantly, we stop living in the past. We proactively choose to take back our power. To be fully present today, we must let go of yesterday. Louise Hay has said that we do not have to know how to forgive; all we have to do is be willing to forgive. We must let the universe take care of the how-to. It has been said that forgiveness is the greatest lesson in life. Until we learn that lesson, true peace will never be ours.

> What seems to us as bitter trials are often lessons in disguise.
>
> —Oscar Wilde

Yesterday is over; we only have today. Why would we allow the negativity of yesterday to contaminate a brand-new day? Why would we want to continue living in all that pain and anguish? We would only be hurting ourselves. By disconnecting from what is over, we can enjoy every present moment and begin to rebuild our lives, finding the value and fulfillment in each precious new moment. There are only two choices in life: we can either move forward or remain stuck in the past.

> Holding on to anger is like grasping a hot coal with the intent of throwing it at someone else; you are the one getting burned.
> —Gautama Buddha (563–483 BC)

There is mounting evidence that the act of forgiveness has emotional and physical payoffs. Research has concluded that when one does not forgive and chooses to hold on to bitterness, anger, hostility, hatred, and resentment, there are physiological consequences, including increased blood pressure, immune suppression, impaired neurological functioning, and a weakening of memory. The unwillingness to forgive affects our energy levels and mood and is linked to cardiovascular disease. Carrying anger, hatred, and resentment has a severe impact on your physical being. A well-known researcher at East Carolina University, Dr. Kathleen Lawyer-Row, states that when people resist forgiving, they also resist the acceptance of what happened. She goes on to say, "If they stay angry, they think they can somehow undo the past." We must contrast this with the people who understand the benefits of forgiving. The forgivers accept the reality of their own experiences, which in turn increases their coping skills and ultimately results in better emotional health. By releasing resentments, we are gifted with a measurable decrease of stress and depression. As if that weren't enough, our levels of physical health and happiness are greatly boosted as well.

Have you ever met someone who is so angry about things that happened in his or her past (e.g., divorce, death, or sibling rivalries) that he or she can't focus on the present, let alone plan for the future? This is what happens when you cannot forgive yourself and others. Don Miguel Ruiz, popular *New York Times* best-selling author, tells us that forgiveness cleans the emotional wounds. By choosing to forgive those who have hurt us, we forgive because we choose not to suffer every time we remember. Ruiz explains, in his book *The Mastery of Love*,

When you can touch a wound and it doesn't hurt, then you know you have truly forgiven. Forgive others, and you will see miracles start to happen in your life. Forgive yourself also—for everything you have done in your whole life. When you forgive yourself, self-acceptance begins and self-love grows. That is the supreme forgiveness—when you finally forgive yourself.

Are You Judgmental?

Over the years, in my coaching practice, I've asked the following question of my clients: "Do you want to be right, or do you want to be happy?" You always have a choice.

Our ego wants to be right, feel superior, and believe we are perfect. We often believe, "I am innocent; therefore, you are guilty. I am a victim; therefore, you are a victimizer." As we maintain a level of self-righteous anger, we suffer; our ego will never allow us to attain inner peace. Thus, choosing to be happy rather than right is the best way to go. When we are happy we can be centered, loving, and self-confident. We live in the present, enjoying our lives to the hilt. As the Buddha has expressed, "Learn to let go. That is the key to happiness."

The problem is that if we live in our heads, we judge. We will never be able to release the toxic emotions of hurt, anger, resentment, sadness, and anxiety when we are thinking and judging. To be a forgiving person means you cease judging. When you stop judging, you go from your head into your gut, the source of all feelings. We cannot feel and think at the same time, so here again, we have the choice to reach deep within, discover and identify our feelings, and then express them in a beneficial way. The reason people often carry grudges, sometimes forever, is because they are still judging and blaming one another. Like cats chasing their tails, they go around and around and only see the situation from one point of view: their own.

New York Times best-selling author Iyanla Vanzant asserts,

> "Forgiveness allows us to explore and release our long-held beliefs and assumptions about ourselves instead of judging other people. The reward of forgiveness is that it eliminates the trap of unconscious ego gratification that we receive when we judge others and give rise to a deeper experience of self-understanding."

Blaming thoughts produce protective walls that create barriers and isolation. The presence of these walls makes healing impossible. They block learning, reciprocity, and any new growth. Negative thoughts are the weeds of your emotional and spiritual garden. They will kill all the beauty, joy, and love in your soul.

As the famous Dr. Wayne Dyer once stated,

"At the root of virtually all spiritual practice is the notion of forgiveness. Think about every single person who has ever harmed you, cheated you, defrauded you, or said unkind things about you. Your experience of them is nothing more than a thought that you carry around with you. These thoughts of resentment, anger and hatred represent slow, debilitating energies that will disempower you. If you could release them, you would know more peace. You practice forgiveness for two reasons: to let others know that you no longer wish to be in a state of hostility with them and to free yourself from the self-defeating energy of resentment. Send love in some form to those you feel have wronged you and notice how much better you feel."

> When you choose to forgive those who have hurt you, you take away their power.
> —Dr. Joy Pedersen

Learning how to forgive takes a bit of practice. All that is required in the beginning is a willingness to forgive. Being willing starts when we make a conscious decision to do some forgiveness work. Begin by declaring, "I intend to forgive." Using that declarative sentence will set your psyche in motion to begin the release of the negative energy from the past. It helps to remember that at some time, in some way, someone once forgave you. Looking at it from that perspective helps you to see forgiveness as a gift that was given to you. You have the choice to pay it forward. For many decades, my coaching clients have found the following exercise to be helpful in closing the door to the past and opening the door to the future.

Forgiveness Exercises

- Begin by writing a letter or note to the person who has offended, hurt, or betrayed you.

- This letter is for you. It will not be mailed or given to your ex or the person who injured you.
- The purpose of the letter is to express your feelings and, in doing so, face and resolve your feelings.
- In this letter, you must include the statement "I forgive you, [name of person who hurt you], for [action that hurt you]."
- Write down the thoughts that come to mind. Write those that come easily and just flow.
- Find a quiet place where you can contemplate and let nature and your spirit guide you.
- Do not think about it. Just let the stream of consciousness take you wherever it's going to take you.
- Say or write the following:
  - I am angry because …
  - I am hurt because …
  - I am sad because …
  - What I would have done differently is …
  - I will always remember … [something positive]
  - I learned …
  - I appreciate the fact that …
  - Thank you for … and being there during …
  - Thank you for …
- Close your letter with "My wish for you is …"

- This letter will acknowledge the time you spent together as a couple.
- Being willing to change and forgive leads to wanting to change and forgive.
- Forgiveness is a gift that you give yourself and that will continue to help you during your life's journey.

I caution my clients that what you send out comes back to you multiplied. It is the law of attraction. Therefore, think carefully about what you say and the wish you send to your ex. Most of my clients choose to repeat this exercise more than once to attain emotional completion. This exercise helps them to move from resentment, hurt, and anger (low vibrational feelings) to a much higher vibrational level created by acceptance, gratitude, and kindness. This will generate good feelings and bring you peace.

Debbie Ford, author of *Spiritual Divorce*, said, "The consequence of refusing to forgive is that we block ourselves from receiving unknown gifts. It is extremely difficult to feel our own self-worth when we are burdened with resentments. What we do to others, we do to ourselves." None of us ever dreamed of growing up as an angry, resentful person. When we were kids, we lived in the moment, enjoying happiness and bliss. By holding on to your resentments, you move away from happiness and joy. You move away from integrity and sabotage your self-respect and self-worth, unintentionally punishing yourself.

Dr. Deepak Chopra, a physician and foremost pioneer in integrative medicine, in his book *Grow Younger, Live Longer*, states, "Whenever you carry resentment, hostility, regret or grievances in your heart, your vitality is eroded."

Dr. Chopra goes on to say, "Studies have shown that journaling about upsetting emotional experiences can improve your immune function, as well as help you gain clarity and insight." When you are journaling, you should use positive words and avoid using negative words and phrases, such as saying someone dumped you, abused you, neglected you, and the like. Focus on expressing the emotions that you felt or still feel. Dr. Chopra also recommends that you should perform some physical ritual to help you release the toxic emotions. Afterward, you should focus on positive kinetic movements (dancing, singing, deep breathing, etc.) to refocus your energy. Many of my clients have found great value in pounding on a pillow, stomping on the ground, or walking or running vigorously to release frustrations and anxiety. These expressive actions yield impressive results.

> *When you recognize that your emotions, as well as others', can be capricious at times, you are better able to forgive and forget.*
>
> —Deepak Chopra, MD

When we peel back the layers, we often find an enormous sense of freedom as we forgive our partner and ourselves. At an unconscious level, we have blamed ourselves for putting up with poor behavior or perhaps allowing what we permitted. Often, we are angry with *ourselves* for our part in whatever happened. Perhaps we looked the other way. Perhaps we didn't speak up or set boundaries. It is possible we even poured gasoline on a fire. When we become emotionally naked with ourselves, we are then able to honestly look at the part we played. When we forgive ourselves, we are indeed free.

When we have forgiven, we make a strong decision to cut the remaining cords of a dead relationship. Forgiveness allows us to heal and end our own suffering and pain. It takes a lot of psychic energy to review and talk about the painful things that led us to the decision of letting go and moving on.

Oftentimes, we are afraid that if we let go and forgive, we are likely to forget, or at least suppress our memories of, those events and then repeat the behavior again and again. If you don't forgive, that is exactly what will happen because the law of attraction will draw a similar situation to you. Let me explain. If you fear getting hurt or disappointed again, that is exactly what you will call into your life (you will attract what you think about). When you forgive, you will chase out the negative thoughts and feelings, which are considered low energy. You will replace them with positive thoughts and feelings, which are high-vibrational positive energy. This will attract the same type of energetic frequency into your life. Like attracts like.

In summation, the main points to keep in mind are as follows:

- Forgiving others is a precious gift you can choose to give yourself.
- There is mounting evidence that you will derive both emotional and physical health benefits from the act of forgiveness.
- Forgiveness does not mean to pardon or sanction another's unacceptable behavior; it simply means to release yesterday to be free today.

- Seeing a hurtful incident through a new perspective leads to healthy detachment, neutrality, and, ultimately, healing.
- Since everything happens for a reason, we can choose to focus on the opportunity for an invaluable lesson, which creates awareness, growth, and wisdom.
- There are valuable lessons to be gleaned from the people and experiences we interact with. When we focus on releasing the past, we will enjoy a life filled with peace, love, and gratitude.

When you forgive, and let go, not only does a huge weight drop off your shoulders, but the doorway to your own self-love opens.

—Louise Hay

Chapter 9

Meditation—There's More Than One Way

> Your vision will become clear only when you look into your heart. Who looks outside, dreams. Who looks inside, awakens.
>
> —Carl Jung

We all want to be calm, centered, and peaceful. Meditation will get you there. The practice of meditation is simple. There are countless ways of getting centered and being in the moment. It is easy to do. It begins with declaring your intention to be calm and peaceful.

For those just getting started, try the following exercise. Find a quiet place to sit and close your eyes. Focus on your body and make yourself comfortable. Begin by noticing each breath. Inhale slowly and deeply while counting to eight. Pause. Slowly exhale through your mouth, counting to nine or ten. It is important to create an exhalation breath slightly longer than your inhalation breath. Slow down your breathing, and your thoughts will also slow down. If this is new to you, practicing meditation for three to five minutes daily will be of great benefit. After a week or two, gradually increase to six or seven minutes. It is important to do your breathing every day; consistent practice yields the best results.

The answers to all your questions are deep within. Meditation will help you get them. All you need to do is connect to your inner wisdom. This process of inward connecting to wisdom goes back thousands of years. There is an old saying: "When you pray, you talk to God. When you meditate, God talks to you." At any rate, all the answers to all the questions are within you. This going within yields a wonderful access to the power that we all carry. Most of us are too busy to notice; we erroneously believe that if we do more, we will feel better. Nothing could be further from the truth. There are many ways to meditate. There is no wrong way to meditate. It is all about being silent and listening to your inner voice.

Since peace and connection to your inner self and divine guidance are created by calming and quieting your mind, make it a priority to spend time every day going within. It will pay dividends beyond your imagination. Ideas, solutions, and other aspects of creativity suddenly emerge as you become an open channel for divine guidance

Here is another example of how to meditate. Begin by sitting in a comfortable chair. Now take three relaxing breaths as you close your eyes. As you exhale, imagine that you are letting go of everything you don't need in your life. Say to yourself, "I am letting go of all anxiety. I am now letting go of all feelings and events that are in the past. I am letting go of all financial worry. I am letting go of all sad feelings, feelings of guilt, or regret about yesterday." You can adjust the emotions given in this example to fit your life and circumstances.

This is the perfect time for releasing and letting go of old patterns in your life that no longer serve you. After doing this for a few minutes, visualize and imagine that every time you are breathing in, you breathe in new life energy. This new energy contains all that you could possibly desire: health, peace, strength, endurance, and unconditional love. With every inhalation, breathe in this new life energy, seeing it as a color—whatever color comes to mind is the best one to go with.

For example, you might see the color gold. Now, as you inhale this gold, say, "I am now happy, lovable, and blessed. I am complete. All is well." Say this five to ten times, and then slowly and gently open your eyes. You are now re-creating your life. The final phrase is "I am now open to my highest good. All is well." Say this last phrase three times, open your eyes, and come back to the room.

> Listen not to the negative words of the others. Listen only to the voice of truth from within. Then follow your heart.
> —Marlene J. Waldock

Plan to spend time every day going within. During times of transition and change, when everything seems chaotic, meditation is an invaluable tool to reclaim your inner peace. By making the decision to connect to a daily practice of meditation, you will have a way to reduce your stress and maximize the inner peace you so richly deserve. It was meditation that helped me make creative and empowering choices during the most tumultuous time in my life: my divorce.

When we meditate, we seek the beautiful, magnificent stillness that lives beyond our thoughts. Thus, whenever we turn within, we visit a place of stillness and peace, which allows us to connect with divine guidance. By connecting with this internal stillness, we're able to observe our thoughts and emotions. This invaluable time allows us to reconnect with ourselves and get centered. We can focus on our breathing and truly be in the moment.

To be in the moment is simple. Being is about suspending any expectations or judgments. Another way to be is to sit quietly as you say, "Now I am going within. Now I am choosing to breathe and just be." Remember to have your feet flat on the floor and your hands in a comfortable position (on your thighs or on the armrests of your chair with your palms up) as you close your eyes and begin. Take a few long, slow, deep breaths. Feel your breath. See it as a beautiful colored vapor that enters your body through the top of your head and then exits out from your heart. Send this beautiful colored vapor out into the world, benefitting others as you exhale and release this vapor. Put all your awareness on the inflow and outflow of your breath.

Your attention might wander, which is common. Imagine your intrusive thoughts as butterflies. These butterflies are simply flying by and will soon move on. Allow the butterflies to just float by. Gently return to your breathing. Some people find it helpful to say, "I am breathing in, and I am breathing out." There is no right or wrong way to meditate. Your intention is to calm your mind, quiet the inner chatter, and find peace.

Meditations are like snowflakes; no two are exactly alike. Therefore, no worries about making a mistake. What is most important is to commit five minutes or so every day. If possible, it is helpful to do it at the same time every day so it becomes a habit. The results are cumulative. The more you do it, the greater the benefits.

I frequently get asked the question "Can I meditate while gardening [or fishing, painting, sculpting, and the like]?" The answer is a definite yes! You must remember to breathe while making a conscious decision to be in the moment; you must have present-moment awareness. You will find yourself feeling happy and serene with a smile both inward as well as outward. There are a variety of ways to make this connection to your inner world; you will find that there are countless benefits of turning inward and practicing present-moment awareness.

You may also choose to meditate by closing your eyes or half closing them in a relaxed way. Say a favorite mantra, such as "Love," "Peace," "I am," or whatever pleases you. Many people find it beneficial to focus on and stare at a fish tank while deliberately slowing their breathing. Others love to sit outdoors and passively look at a garden or a beach, breathing in the delightful aromas that surround them and possibly tuning in to the sounds of birds chirping or listening to the breaking waves at the shore. Additionally, there is always the option of staring at the rain or gazing passively at a burning fire while breathing slowly in through the nose and deliberately out through the mouth. People choose what they consider to be the most calming and centering. Often, when taking a walk, I will choose a meditative walk. On my way out, I concentrate on my breathing and look around to notice the many things I find particularly beautiful or special. I enjoy the feeling of peaceful gratitude. On my way back home, using my ten fingers, I do a round of "I am grateful for ..." I am often inspired to do two or three rounds as I count the many things the universe has given me. I call this a moving meditation. Over the years, I have shared this practice with a great number of people who find it works well in helping them feel uplifted and centered.

I do whatever I need to do to keep my inner world peaceful. My inner peace is essential for my health and well-being.
—Louise Hay

Benefits of Meditation

The following are some benefits of meditation:

- increased self-awareness
- increased ability to become inspired
- ability to access creativity
- more peace
- more openness
- more creativity
- more flexibility
- more trust
- more resourcefulness
- more love
- more optimism
- lower blood pressure

> In today's rush, we all think too much, seek too much and want too much and forget about the joy of just being.
> —Eckart Tolle

Peacefulness increases radically as you surrender to the here and now. Meditation is a fabulous way to reduce stress. There are infinite possibilities as you learn to trust yourself more fully and tune in to your inner world. Finding this beautiful place within unlocks serenity, power, and bliss. It not only enables you to tune in to your intuition, a valid source of information and inner guidance, but also increases self-awareness. You can practice meditation anywhere and at any time. The only requirement is your intention to be calm.

My own daily routine starts while sitting in the tub. I close my eyes, concentrate, and slow down my breathing. I like using the word *love* as I visualize a metronome clicking back and forth. When I have invading thoughts, I picture them as butterflies and let them gently make their way across my horizon. By meditating in the morning, I notice that my entire day unfolds in beautiful ways, making me the recipient of many miracles and much creativity. I also make it a habit to meditate in the evening as part of my nightly routine. I have found that I sleep much better.

Learn to be in touch with the silence within yourself and know that everything in life has a purpose. There are no mistakes, all events are blessings given to us to learn from.

—Dr. Elisabeth Kubler-Ross

Chapter 10

The Power of Gratitude

The word *gratitude* is derived from the Latin word *gratia*, which means "greatness," "graciousness," or "gratefulness." Gratitude is a thankful appreciation for what we receive, be it tangible or intangible. When we are grateful, we acknowledge the goodness in our lives. To live from a place of gratitude can be life transforming.

I first realized this many years ago while at the airport. As it turned out, I had arrived too late to board my flight. No worries—I was assured there was room on the next flight. To pass the time, I found myself wandering to a nearby coffee shop. While sipping on my delicious cappuccino, I took out my notebook. Somehow, I was inspired to make a list of things in my life I was grateful for. I decided to make two lists: one for the external things and one for the internal things. For example, on my external page, I wrote that I was grateful for my four wonderful children and my loving husband. I was also grateful for my dependable car, my lovely home, my wonderful private practice, and the many opportunities to travel. The internal list noted that I felt grateful for my healthy body, sharp and creative mind, excellent memory, enthusiasm, intelligence, compassion, warmth, and so on. This made me feel so good; since I was on a roll, I kept going. In a short time, I covered several pages as my list went on and on.

I wanted to acknowledge the many people I knew who believed in me, inspired me, helped me in some way, saw the good in me, and loved me. These people had touched my life, and by just recalling them, I felt tremendous gratitude and love. I remember recalling my godmother, who lived in New York City. She taught me the meaning of unconditional love. I could always look to her for encouragement and support. She was one of my greatest teachers.

Anita, my best friend for many years, who came to the United States from Ecuador, touched my life in many ways. She taught me how to be compassionate, patient, nonjudgmental, and forgiving. These were huge lessons I learned through her behavior and encouragement. I would not have become a teacher or had the confidence to move into the field of mental health had it not been for my beautiful, loving friend.

As I went back in time, I recalled an extraordinary man who influenced and inspired me. Dr. John DeVoy had been my oral surgeon and ultimately a dear friend. Through his belief in me, I had the courage and conviction to get out of my comfort zone, take many risks, further my education, and get my master's degree in counseling.

That time in my life was a time of enormous growth and change. I learned what the word *passionate* meant as I moved forward in my life. Through writing this gratitude list, I began to recall many kind and inspirational people who touched my life and affected me. I came to see that there were no coincidences; the power of intention was truly strong and effective, and everything happened for a reason.

After I finished my gratitude lists, miracles began to happen. I returned to the boarding area and was told I had been upgraded to first class. I was overjoyed! It was the first time I ever flew in first class.

Onboard, I struck up a conversation with the woman sitting next to me and found that we had many things in common. It felt as if we had known each other all our lives! We even happened to live in the same town. We shared so much that we developed a friendship. She is still a cherished and valued friend, and we often laugh about our meeting.

When I got to the hotel, the universe blessed me once again, and I was offered an upgrade from my standard room. I received a gorgeous suite with a breathtaking view. The flowers, candy, and sparkling water filled me with overwhelming gratitude. It soon occurred to me that these miraculous gifts had appeared following the gratitude lists I had created. I sensed the connection between feeling grateful and attracting miracles into my life. This inspired me to complete a gratitude list every evening. It is a habit that has become a part of my life to this day. I strongly encourage you, the reader, to make it a part of your life too.

Dr. Albert Einstein stated, almost a hundred years ago, "Everything is Energy and that's really all there is to it. Match the frequency of the reality you want and you cannot help but get that reality. It can be no other way. This is not Philosophy. This is Physics."

During the last several decades, it has been scientifically documented that the way you think affects your vibrational energy. In other words, the thoughts you think will either make you feel happy or make you feel scared, worried, insecure, anxious, angry, etc. Your thoughts will either raise your vibrational energy or bring your energy way down. When you say things to yourself like "What if I fail?" or "What if I make a fool of myself?" these thoughts will lower your energy, as they are based on fear, and fear is a negative emotion.

These sentence stems are a small sampling to increase your vibrational energy:

- I am grateful for …
- I'm so lucky to have the opportunity …
- I feel good about …
- I'm happy about …
- I appreciate the …
- I am so enjoying the …

Numerous studies have shown that keeping a daily gratitude journal has long-lasting effects on happiness as well as overall physical health. Research has shown that gratitude appears to be the strongest link to health and happiness. Dr. Martin Seligman found that the positive effects of being gratitude-focused (e.g., writing a letter of appreciation, etc.) had a profound positive effect that lasted up to one month. Dr. Seligman, former president of the American Psychological Association, published his findings in the *Journal of American Psychology.*

We all know that saying thank you is a sign of good manners but showing appreciation can also result in finding and winning new friends. According to a 2014 study published in *Emotion*, new acquaintances were more likely to seek an ongoing relationship when you held a door, sent a thank-you note, or verbally acknowledged their kindness.

> Cultivate the habit of being grateful for every good thing that comes to you, and give thanks continuously. And because of all the things that have contributed to your advancement, you should include all things in your gratitude.
> —Ralph Waldo Emerson

Alan Cohen, workshop leader, speaker, and author of numerous best-selling books, has declared,

> We attract to us that which we think. If we think and see goodness and prosperity, they shall come to us. If we dwell upon negativity and suffering, that is what we will find. We are constantly attracting to us people and conditions that mirror exactly our patterns of thought.

If we are in a room with positive, happy people, we get good feelings just by being near them. We become uplifted as we enjoy the energy they create. Being in their presence makes us feel good. When people think grateful, optimistic thoughts, their positive vibrations are received by all who are nearby. Their dynamism is contagious! That's why we love to be close to those who are vibrating positive energy. The eminent Cheryl Richardson, renowned life coach, says, "Count your blessings. A grateful heart attracts more joy, love and prosperity."

By contrast, we can all think of people who deplete our energy. They look at the negative side of everything; they are constant complainers. When asked if they enjoyed their vacation, the first thing they mention is how the airline lost a piece of their luggage or how it rained for the first few days. By focusing on what was disappointing, they erase and minimize the many positives. For example, they forget to mention that they were upgraded on their flight, made a new friend or won first prize in the bike competition or that the hotel had the most amazing workout room ever.

Alan Cohen writes,

> We must respect the power of thoughts,
> for they can make us or break us. We do
> not create our lives from nothing, but we

certainly set into motion the events that create circumstances. By the time we see a circumstance, we are seeing the effect of a series of events that began with a thought a long time ago.

Alan goes on to say, "We cannot allow ourselves the luxury of an 'idle' thought as there is no such thing. Every thought is a seed. What we plant in our mental garden will grow."

All words you speak have a frequency, and the moment you speak or think them, their energy is released into the universe. The law of attraction responds to all frequencies and will respond to the energy you release. When you use strong words, such as *terrible*, *shocking*, and *horrible*, to describe any situation in life, you will be sending out an equally strong frequency, and the law of attraction must respond by bringing back that frequency to you. It is indiscriminate. We attract people who mirror our vibrational frequency and are in vibrational harmony with us. When we change our energy, our new thoughts and feelings will impact our outside world as well. Thus, relationships will not continue to work the same way if one partner changes by growing and the other does not. A good example is people who are primarily anxious and operate out of fear. To lessen their anxiety, they try to control everything and everyone around them. Once they have chosen to work on the issues in counseling, they stop living in the future and give up the idea they have control over their external world. They realize that what they focus on increases and expands. Through their awareness, they become internally focused rather than externally focused. They learn how they are responsible for the reality they create. As they focus on being grateful and start living in the present, they take back their power. They change their thoughts into positive energy and affirmations. Gratitude is accepting, allowing, and appreciating all that is. Gratitude is knowing that whatever happens, nothing happens accidentally. Often, we do not initially understand or see the golden nugget—that is, the gifts and enriching lessons given to us.

The law of attraction is beautifully explained in the best-selling book *Ask and It Is Given* by Esther and Jerry Hicks. The book states,

> Every thought vibrates, every thought radiates a signal, and every thought attracts a matching signal back. We call that process *The Law of Attraction*. The *Law of Attraction* says: *That which is like unto itself is drawn* and so you might see the powerful *Law of Attraction* as a

sort of Universal Manager that sees to it that all thoughts that match one another line up.

Clearly, we can understand how the law of attraction is the most powerful law in the universe.

If you feel good, you'll attract others who feel good. Additionally, you will attract other experiences that feel good. Hence, it is very important to raise your vibrational frequency. Positive feelings, such as joy, love, and gratitude, are of a high frequency. Negative feelings, such as fear, guilt, and self-pity, send out low-frequency vibrations. Like attracts like. It's all about the energy, known as our frequency or our vibration.

According to Rhonda Byrne, an expert on the law of attraction and best-selling author of *The Power,* "Every single second is an opportunity to change your life, because in any moment you can change the way you feel. It doesn't matter what you have felt before." It doesn't matter what mistakes you think you have made. When you change the way you feel, you are on a different frequency, and the law of attraction responds instantaneously. When you change the way you feel, the past has gone! When you change the way you feel, your life changes.

Rhonda Byrne continues in *The Power*, "The better you feel, the better life gets." When we decide we are going to be grateful and focus on the positive, our lives become more and more fulfilling as we attract what we need, want, and desire.

In my own life, I use a thought pattern that I learned from Louise Hay. When uncomfortable, tense, or anxious moments approach in my life, I begin a short session of deep breathing and then visualize a rainbow of light being projected from my heart at the source of my anxiety. For example, I use this technique before I visit the dentist. Then I affirm, "I send love ahead. I send love ahead." Typically, I say this affirmation five to ten times while visualizing my projected rainbow. My process immediately makes me feel calm, peaceful, and centered. I usually add, "All is well; this situation has a happy ending. I am grateful."

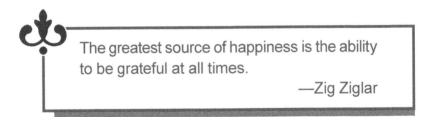

The greatest source of happiness is the ability to be grateful at all times.

—Zig Ziglar

Before you love again, it is imperative that you embrace change and gratitude. Most importantly, you should show gratitude to yourself.

Chapter 11

The Seven Cs of a Happy Relationship

Chemistry

For well over three decades, relationship research psychologists have studied the origin and importance of chemistry on a couple's predictors of happiness. What is chemistry really? How important is it in a couple's relationship? What is going on inside of us when we are in love? How are we affected?

Unlike Frank Sinatra, who asks in the popular song "How Little We Know," "Who cares to define what chemistry this is? Who cares with your lips on mine how ignorant bliss is?" We need to know the seven Cs if we are to have an enduring relationship. We need to understand how important this chemistry is in a couple's relationship.

Chemistry can be seen as the magic that happens when two people are profoundly attracted to one another.

In my practice, I have heard countless couples declare, "It was love at first sight!" or "It was magical!" People can be magnetized by each other's voice, smell, face, or body. The brain produces various chemicals that affect our behavior. When there is a strong physical attraction, the brain produces large amounts of a chemical called dopamine. Dopamine causes a quickened heartbeat and intense feelings of pleasure, ecstasy, and happiness. Dopamine will sweep you away in a euphoric state of passion while heightening your level of energy along with providing a feeling of tremendous exhilaration. Novelty also stimulates the production of dopamine. Therefore, having sex with a new partner, interacting with a new partner, or even thinking about a new partner can cause sexual arousal and pleasure. The brain is happy to supply this delicious chemical, which explains why affairs can be so tempting. Dopamine will rob you of your senses and logic and put stars in your eyes. Dr. Holly Hein, psychologist, relationship expert, and author of the popular book *Sexual Detours*, calls this initial attraction phase the infatuation stage of a relationship.

During the infatuation stage, we think of our partners constantly; they are on our minds throughout the day and night. We are restless and pine for them when we are apart. We are sure this connection is the real thing. *Why, this must be love!* During this stage of our relationship, we idealize our love objects. Emotions run high; we are in a state of bliss. We are in a dream state and enraptured; we are on an emotional roller coaster—and damn, it feels good. We are under the influence of dopamine, although we believe we are in love. It feels so fabulous that someone finds us irresistible and believes we are the answer to a prayer. Romantic love is intense. It is based on passion and illusion.

As lovely as it is, we must remember that this is a fantasy. It is not reality. You might recognize the following words from "Hey There," a song popularized by Rosemary Clooney and written by Georg C. Dolvio and Greg Fields: "Hey there, you with the stars in your eyes. Love never made a fool of you; you used to be so wise."

Millions of people related to those words and wanted to know "if they were too much in love to hear, or was it all going in one ear and out the other?" The perverse effect of dopamine is that we recognize and know what happens under its influence, but frankly, we don't care.

When I lecture on love to my college students, a question I pose to them is "Would you attempt to reconcile your checking account after you had too much alcohol?" We know that our judgment is clouded in such a situation, so the answer is always no. Yet during the infatuation phase of a relationship, we set unrealistic expectations, idolize our partners, and see only the best. We see them as being perfect and not having any faults. When we do recognize a fault, we minimize it so it does not disrupt the fantasy that they are perfect for us. Dopamine is so powerful that we can blind ourselves to reality and create a romantic illusion.

When two people are in the throes of dopamine, sleep often takes a backseat. It is common for couples to stay up half the night talking, having sex, and laughing with and enjoying each other's presence. There is never enough time to be together. People even lose their appetites, and you often hear comments like "Wow, Melissa never looked so good!"

Another interesting phenomenon during the infatuation stage is that people step out of their normal behavioral comfort zones. A person who is generally careful about money (the saver) now spends money with a newfound level of happiness and confidence. Often, the shy person will become demonstrative and talkative. An abrupt, sarcastic person might become more open, more trusting, and kinder. Heather, an administrative assistant, was fond of saying, "It was a pleasure to work with my boss after the dopamine cocktail kicked in. A workaholic to the tenth degree, he stopped coming in to the office; it was paradise!"

For those going through it, the infatuation phase creates feelings of euphoria. Life has new meaning. The words of poets and love songs now make sense, and the world is a lovelier place. People might say things like the following to try to describe the effect:

- He lost his head.
- She's mad about him.
- He's crazy in love.
- She's walking on cloud nine.
- He's been bitten by the love bug.
- She's head over heels for him.

These expressions, and many more, depict people who have thrown reason and common sense out the window. They are blinded by romantic bliss.

Dr. Pat Love, author and relationship expert, writes in *The Truth about Love*, "When you look at societies with the least stable marriages and the highest divorce rates, they are the ones that use the infatuation phase as the sole or major criterion for marriage." In other words, infatuation and relationship longevity do not correlate. They can, but they generally do not.

In her books about love and relationships, Dr. Pat Love states, "Infatuation is nature's way of getting you to meet, mate, procreate and produce healthy offspring." This is the driving force of nature and your raison d'être, or reason for being. Mother Nature has only given us a limited time to stay in that euphoric state—approximately two or three years. After that time, the effects of the dopamine cocktail end, and the euphoria declines as we begin to sober up. The feeling that you can't live without him or her, the long talks till the wee hours, the loss of appetite, the electrifying kiss, and the feeling that you have won the lottery end. As we realize the honeymoon phase is over, we move to the next stage of our relationship. Unless we are aware of the transient nature of the chemistry, disillusion will set in, and we will not move to the next level.

Dr. Holly Hein states,

> In real life, love, sex, marriage and intimacy are far more complicated and confusing … We must draw a line between the euphoria of romantic love and the reality of creating intimacy.

> Romantic love inhibits intimacy because romance is based on illusion and intimacy is based on reality.

Incidentally, affairs usually die out when the dopamine stops and the illusion phase is over. My research on famous people who have had multiple marriages reveals that the couples began to have troubles just about the time the dopamine declined. The failure of these relationships came about because they lacked the skills necessary for continued intimacy, never realizing that sex is not intimacy. Sex, enhanced by dopamine, is like whipped cream on top of the cake. It looks good and tastes great but is not nutritious and will not sustain you.

This is not to say there is no longer chemistry between the partners. Oxytocin, also secreted by the brain, is a chemical that promotes bonding, relaxation, security, and trust. These are the qualities needed for a deeper appreciation of our partners and are vital for closeness and healthy attachment. Oxytocin is also known as the cuddle hormone, the love hormone, or the bliss hormone.

Oxytocin makes us more sensitive to the emotions and needs of another. It encourages us to be more empathetic and supportive. Mature couples navigate through the transition from dopamine to oxytocin as they continue to appreciate their partners' gifts. Mature couples also have realistic expectations. They realize there is no perfect partner or perfect relationship. They are accepting and focus on the positive and not the negative. Building a foundation of trust, appreciation, respect, and mutual sharing is necessary to create a long-lasting and fulfilling relationship.

According to a study published in *The Journal of Neuroscience*, when men were given the hormone oxytocin, they were more likely to stay away from attractive women they didn't know and remain faithful in a monogamous relationship. Rene Hurleman, MD, from the University of Bonn, Germany, explained it this way: "Previous animal research in prairie voles identified oxytocin as the major key for monogamous fidelity in animals. Here, we provide the first evidence that oxytocin may have a similar role in humans."

Medical researchers have discovered that oxytocin helps to reduce the stress hormone cortisol as well. Cortisol prepares the body for flight or fight. It activates all systems and creates hypervigilance, stress, and anxiety. Oxytocin not only counters the effects of cortisol but also reduces stress and helps enable our relationships to flourish. We produce oxytocin by kissing, touching, holding hands, petting an animal, or even having an orgasm.

When two friends look into each other's eyes, are totally present for one another, and speak from their hearts, this stimulates the production of even more oxytocin. Secure attachment is created when two lovers appreciate, cherish, and nurture their deep friendship. The sharing and trusting will replace the dopamine cocktail, thus deepening the bonds between them.

Compatibility

Compatibility is another one of the seven Cs. There are countless couples who turned lust into love, had good communication skills, and were committed to being together but discovered they were not compatible. It is essential to know what you are looking for in a partner. More importantly, do you know the must-haves you seek? They represent who you are and what really matters. We need to be clear and honest about what we will and will not compromise on. Our priorities are the things that matter most, such as money, sophistication, good looks, good grammar, good manners, ambition, education, status, reliability, humor, warmth, authenticity, honesty, kindness, humility, loyalty, a love for the outdoors, family life, charity, good communication skills, and neat personal habits, to mention just a few.

Mark always loved family life and made it a priority. His vision was to have a dog and a large piece of property and raise a brood of children. He downplayed his dreams with Alexandra and never fully shared his dreams early on. During their passionate two-year relationship, they learned a great many things about one another. When Mark moved in with Alexandra, he finally began expressing his dreams about family, relationships, and kids. While Alexandra agreed that kids were special (she enjoyed being with her older sisters' children), she also explained to Mark the passion she had for traveling and adventure.

During their time together, she introduced Mark to a great many outdoor sports, such as hiking and whitewater rafting. They took many adventure-style vacations together. However, when they spent time with Mark's family, Alexandra felt that she didn't fit in and began to disconnect and distance herself. She realized that some of her core values were to spend time in nature and experience adventure.

They ended their relationship when it became clear the kind of life Mark wanted was not compatible with the kind of life she wanted. His vision centered on family life; hers centered on other pursuits.

Additionally, Alexandra began complaining about Mark's disorganization. He left dishes around and dropped his clothes wherever they fell. Alexandra, who was fastidious, liked to have things neat and organized. Anything less than that made her anxious.

Because of their differences, this couple made the decision that their values and goals were not compatible. They ended their relationship under favorable circumstances, realizing that they had no future.

Larry and Samantha also had clashing values. Larry's parents always had lived a larger-than-life existence. They were well off and made a lot of money. They lived a life of luxury, enjoyed their wealth, and had many material comforts. Larry had been given an expensive car for his seventeenth birthday and had had a generous allowance, which he'd always spent. His parents had not given him boundaries, nor had they questioned his purchases.

Samantha came from a family that worked hard for everything they had. The family motto was "If you don't have the cash for it, you wait until you do." She worked during her college years and even took extra jobs on weekends. She struggled to pay for her education and took it seriously. She was disciplined about money.

Of course, she was attracted to his impetuous, bon vivant style, and after a whirlwind nine-month courtship, they became engaged. Samantha quickly realized their values were so different that they could not overcome their incompatibility. Additionally, she discovered that Larry's credit had a shockingly low score, and he was not interested in buying a house and settling down.

He balked at the responsibility of being a homeowner and had little respect for money. After relationship counseling, they came to the conclusion that their values were not compatible.

It is essential to know what you are looking for in a partner. More importantly, it is necessary to know what your core values are. Our core values represent who we are and what really matters to us as individuals. We need to be clear and honest about what we will and will not comprise on.

I give my clients a worksheet on which they are instructed to select their top twelve core values from a list. The following is a sampling of the core value list:

- affectionate
- appreciative
- compassionate
- dependable
- emotionally available
- family-oriented
- forgiving
- hardworking
- honest

- humorous
- intelligent
- kind
- loyal
- nonjudgmental
- nurturing
- optimistic
- organized
- passionate
- patient
- protective
- respectful
- responsible
- romantic
- sexy
- spiritual
- successful
- supportive
- thoughtful
- trustworthy

These are some of the choices from the master list. After my clients circle their top twelve, they are then instructed to highlight the five most important of these. This exercise helps my clients be clear about who they are and what their core values are. By doing this, we honor and respect ourselves.

My clients have found it beneficial to get clear on the top five traits, qualities, and behaviors that are important to them in a committed relationship. During the courting phase, I recommend that the couple openly share their top twelve and also their top five with one another.

Caring

Caring means being thoughtful in ways that send a strong message, such as "I love you, and you are important to me." It is vital to let your loved one know you cherish and adore him or her.

What is the essential ingredient that keeps people together over the years? John and Mary, former neighbors of mine, enjoy a secure and loving marriage. They recently celebrated their fiftieth wedding anniversary. Both partners are still involved with their respective careers. He is a pharmacist, and she's an interior designer. They look and act as if they are in their fifties, even though they are in their seventies.

One day during dinner, I asked them what their secret was. John said, "We truly care about one another. I care about Mary's health and happiness, and she cares about mine. We are each other's best friends. There is nothing I wouldn't do for Mary." They looked tenderly at one another as they spoke. Mary added, "John is such a thoughtful man. He is constantly doing things for me to express his kindness and love. He often surprises me with the sweetest of gifts and does a great job of keeping romance alive. I find that he is my best friend. I so appreciate him."

John is an important part of Mary's support network. John scrapes the ice and snow off Mary's car during the frigid days of winter. He also warms up her car as a way of letting her know how much he cares about her. He assumes responsibility for her car to ensure her safety and well-being. He takes it in for service and checks her tires regularly, making sure she has a safe car to drive. Although John is a tea drinker, he brews fresh coffee for Mary each morning. Mary loves feeling pampered and being the recipient of John's attentions and thoughtfulness. She enjoys the feeling of being important to him.

Mary bakes John's favorite brownies or scones on the weekends. They make it a habit to take after-dinner walks and have tea together each evening while they watch TV or read. They regularly give massages to one another and enjoy caring and connecting. Mary is protective of John and assumes the biweekly burden of calling John's aging mother. She is a feisty, opinionated woman who drains

John. John often thanks Mary for relieving him of this responsibility.

One old but relevant definition of love is "caring about someone else's needs as much as your own." Naturally, we all have feelings, wants, and needs. We understand that we are responsible for getting our own needs met. In a committed relationship, we directly and indirectly show our partners that we truly care about their needs as we do our own needs. This caring deepens trust, along with enhancing security and intimacy.

We all know what happens to a garden when it is neglected. The same is true for relationships. When couples become apathetic, the relationship is headed for disaster. An untended garden does not bear fruit or flowers.

When people feel neglected, criticized, or misunderstood, they often erect protective walls. One might say, "My partner doesn't care about me—not really! We've been living like roommates rather than friends or lovers. We've just grown apart over the years."

With much sadness and resignation, each partner points out how much he or she does not feel cared for. They live in an emotionally sterile atmosphere that lacks intimacy and trust. The garden does not receive sunshine and has become barren.

When we respect one another, we don't try to change our partners. We accept them as they are, understanding that every person is unique. We love and cherish them unconditionally—the same way we want to be loved!

When we truly care, we listen attentively to what our partners are saying, using concern and empathy to validate their feelings. We remind them how much we truly care; we build trust and feelings of connectivity as our intimacy grows. When we care about our partners' feelings and reassure them of this, they feel secure, safe, loved, and accepted. Consequently, there is no need to be defensive; there is no need to attack or withdraw from the conversation. We focus on our beloveds' positive qualities, letting them know how much we appreciate and value them. Kindness begets more kindness.

In the fast-paced world in which we live, it is easy for us to become achievement-oriented and forget to let our loved one know how much we care. Leaving a special love note, sending a text, telling our lovers how much we appreciate them, giving them a wink in a crowded room, and letting them know how sexy we find them are just a few ways to prevent stagnation and neglect from settling in. There are countless ways to water and feed your garden if you start with the intention of letting your loved one know how special he or she is and how much he or she means to you. Caring and kindness are powerful ways to enrich a love relationship.

Communication

Good relationships don't just happen; a successful relationship takes two committed people with effective communication skills.

Poor communication is one of the prime reasons for marriages and other relationships to end. The ability to effectively communicate will affect your level of intimacy. The impact of not communicating effectively is that partners feel uncared for, and their sense of safety declines. When this sense of hopelessness increases, partners move further and further away from one another.

Protective walls begin to grow along with unhappiness. At this point, couples feel the relationship is making them miserable. The respect and trust they once felt for one another have vanished. Apathy and hostility increase.

Some people, during the relationship, avoid sharing their true feelings and do not communicate well. This results in their needs not getting met. They often think, *Why bother? Nothing is going to change anyway.*

When both partners incessantly argue and bicker, they are wrapped up in their need to be right. The result is that neither party is listening; instead, they obsess about why their partner is so wrong and why they are so right. Nothing ever gets resolved, and couples live with resentment, contempt, and frustration toward one another.

To break this cycle and increase openness, it is essential to help your partner feel supported. This will increase the depth of communication and make your partner feel understood.

The growth of trust and openness is enhanced by the following:

- being open-minded
- self-disclosing
- being compassionate
- being able to say you are sorry
- having control of your emotions
- being able to identify what you are feeling
- being able to articulate what you are feeling
- having a sincere desire for resolution
- valuing the other person as well as your relationship
- being clear about your core values
- giving validation to your partner's needs and feelings

It is important to stay present when your partner is speaking; using good eye contact and compassion will help your partner feel respected and appreciated. Listening well is one of the major keys to effective communication.

Couples need to feel supported, not judged. Each partner has a right to feel valued and appreciated. The skill of listening well begins by putting aside your own beliefs, anxieties, and self-interest so you can put yourself in the other person's place. Try to look at things from his or her perspective.

Simply being quiet while someone else speaks does not constitute real listening. To be successful at listening, do the following:

1. Be totally present. Maintain good eye contact. Lean slightly forward. From time to time, nod when you agree with something your partner is saying that resonates with you. During times of disagreement, remember that your beloved is not your adversary. Remember, you are partners; you both want to be happy and secure. Research has borne out that couples who respond with respect and kindness have a much greater opportunity to work out their issues during times of disagreement and conflict.

2. Resist the urge to interrupt when your partner is speaking, no matter how tempting it is. Let the other person finish. The conversation is not about being right; it is about resolving an issue with the most important person in your life: your best friend.

3. Give reassurance; don't be dismissive of your partner's feelings or thoughts. Let you partner know that you respect and care about him or her. Remind your partner that your goal is to understand things from his or her point of view. You can say, "I can see why you would be disappointed. Yes, that really is very upsetting. That would have bothered me too."

4. Do not take a defensive approach. When you do, you are pouring gasoline on a burning fire. Defensiveness leads to damage and destruction. Refrain from comments like the following:
   ○ "I don't remember saying that!"
   ○ "No way! You're exaggerating, as you always do!"
   ○ "Well, I didn't do it deliberately!"
   ○ "So? Big deal! I forgot!"
   ○ "Can't you let that go already? I'm getting tired of listening to you go on about such crap!"
   ○ "Well, I'm not perfect! Are you?"

5. Use active listening. Active listening has been used for many decades. I teach my clients how to use this communication skill, which results in deepening the connection between partners. In active listening, you repeat back to your partner, using your own words and sentence structure, the message you think you just heard. To attempt to clarify what you think the other person just said, ask, "Did I get that right?" or "Is that what you meant?" This will not only reassure your partner that you were paying attention but also give you a chance to take in what he or she was saying and remember it.

The messages we send need to be clear. It is not uncommon for people to simply hint at what they really want rather than express themselves directly.

For example, Katie has a problem with lower back pain and was told by her chiropractor not to lift anything heavy. She has just returned with a trunk load of groceries. She begins lifting the heavy bags by herself, hoping John will take the hint as she's moaning and groaning about how heavy the grocery clerk made the bags. John is on the computer and is not paying attention. Katie feels resentful.

Then there is Kyle, a thirteen-year-old boy who retreats to his room every time Mom brings home her new boyfriend. He closes the door with a loud bang, hoping Mom will get the hint about how unhappy he is. Kyle feels worried, left out, and threatened. He hints but does not directly communicate his feelings or concerns.

Many people assume the other person knows how they feel and what they need. Hints are usually unrecognized by the other and, therefore, ignored. The person putting out the hint becomes increasingly resentful and irritated at the other person. All this could be avoided by learning to communicate clearly and effectively and openly saying what we would like. By asking for what we need and expressing what we feel, the bond of trust grows proportionately. This is key for establishing connection and intimacy.

When two people form a partnership, there will inevitably be areas of conflict. That's a given. Begin by finding a peaceful place to have difficult conversations to maximize the impact of your message.

Then make sure that you are well centered and that strong emotions have subsided. Close your eyes and breathe in deeply and slowly as you count to five. Then hold the breath and count to three. Exhale very slowly to the count of seven.

Do this several times. This will activate your parasympathetic nervous system, which will calm you. Finally, remind yourself of your goal.

For example, "I intend to let Vicki know that I felt very uncomfortable and exposed when she announced to the family that my pot smoking led to my flunking out of college. I need to remind myself that she made a mistake; she loves me and did not intend to make me feel small and embarrassed. My goal is to make her aware of my feelings so this will not happen again. I will start with something positive—something I appreciate about her. I will tell her that I'm sure she did not do it intentionally but that it really did bother me."

We must remember that when we are kind, patient, respectful, and understanding, our partners will be too. Our relationships will have more trust, intimacy, and depth.

Intimacy consists of the self-disclosure of personal information and feelings. To attain true intimacy, there needs to be a climate of trust and safety. An emotional atmosphere of kindness, acceptance, and respect will lead to feelings of being safe. People feel safe, one would say, to speak from the heart.

All too often, I've heard one person say to the other, "But you shouldn't feel that way—that's just ridiculous." This type of statement is not only ineffective but also results in the recipient feeling discounted. After all, a feeling cannot be judged as being right or wrong any more than someone saying, "I am too hot or too cold." Feelings are valid. They need to be respected because they are unique to each person. The way people feel is, to them, their intimate truth. For the individual, the perception is the reality, and the reality is the truth.

A better response is to say, "I understand that such and such made you feel hurt and frustrated. I appreciate you sharing that with me." When you validate your partner's feelings, you have taken the first step in heart-to-heart communication. To reinforce trust and closeness, give your partner your complete attention, touch him or her, and softly speak with kindness and sincerity. Say to him or her, "What can I do to make you feel supported and loved? I'm here for you. I truly care about your needs and feelings."

Compassion

Why is compassion an important ingredient for a happy relationship? For intimacy to flourish, make every attempt to understand where the other person is coming from—what it must be like from his or her point of view, given his or her values, background, and current stress level. When one is compassionate, one is also sympathetic, supportive, understanding, nonjudgmental, kind, and forgiving. These qualities create an atmosphere of safety and trust. A compassionate person assumes the best in others and accepts the fact that others make mistakes. Compassion is beneficial not only to the other partner but also to the relationship. It serves to elevate your own self-respect. By being compassionate, you will put yourself in the shoes of the other person.

Bill felt discounted when Laurie, his wife, initially did not respond positively to his "I love you so much" statement. He did not understand that Laurie was preoccupied. Laurie's mother had been taken to the hospital several days earlier and had had open-heart surgery. Bill, the next morning, in a tender voice, said to Laurie, "Are you okay? I tried to communicate with you, but you seemed to be a million miles away. Is there anything I can do?"

This opened an emotional dialogue, with Laurie tearfully explaining that she was worried about her mother's illness and whether or not her mother would survive. Bill was able to reassure Laurie that he was there for her and that somehow, they would get through this major challenge together.

He told Laurie, "I understand how much you love your mom and how difficult this is for you." Rather than dwelling on his feelings of being discounted, Bill took the time to be kind, patient, and compassionate. He communicated not for his own good but for his partner and the relationship. His focus was on Laurie's stress; he pushed his own feelings aside for the moment.

> Part of working on yourself is learning how to support another person in being the best they can be. Partners are meant to help each other access the highest parts within themselves.
> —Marianne Williamson

A compassionate person uses both kindness and humility and is able and willing to apologize. When we offer an apology, we strengthen the bonds that hold the relationship together. People mirror us back. When one partner shows humility and the desire to rebuild and repair the couple's sacred bond, the other partner will be receptive and compassionate as well. He or she too is inspired to hold out the olive branch. The alternative is that the hurt partner will sweep his or her feelings of disappointment and frustration under the rug while accumulating resentments. These resentments fester, grow, and eventually explode. In time, this partner will reach the point of no return and will announce that the relationship is over.

Being able to apologize not only is healthy for the sake of the relationship but also enhances personal growth. Apologizing leads to greater self-esteem as well as increased integrity. Those three little words "I am sorry" can be powerful and pivotal.

It is, of course, necessary for us to be honest with ourselves, particularly about the stories we are running in our heads when we've had a hiccup in our relationship. A story such as "Well, my partner should have known I was under a great deal of stress at work and should not have brought up such a touchy subject" is an example of a story we spin in order to be right.

In Ken Blanchard and Margret McBride's best-selling book *The One Minute Apology*, the authors make the point that it is necessary to surrender to the truth while we are totally open and honest within ourselves.

> To surrender, you must first let go of being right, and then confront the truth about your own failings by being 100% honest with yourself. A fundamental concept to remember is: Kidding yourself is an expensive habit that has no reward. When you surrender, you let go of the story you've told yourself, and realize that you have to apologize to those you have offended, regardless of the outcome.
>
> Ken Blanchard and Margret McBride

In my practice, I have often seen the way couples fight to be right. This never has a happy outcome. This destructive behavior can be avoided when we use compassion and put ourselves in the other person's shoes.

We can be more compassionate when we release our egos. Egos are judgmental and competitive and want to be perfect. In the desire to be right, they want to be in control and care about what other people think, say, and do. It is the ego that wants to hold on to past hurts and disappointments.

By giving up judgmental thoughts, we will be able to go from our heads to our hearts. The heart is our doorway to divine guidance and intuition. As we use heart energy, we stay in a love-based relationship rather than a thought-based relationship. Heart energy is about forgiveness and seeks to forgive; it feels better when we let go of old grievances and move forward. Heart energy uses compassion to be understanding and will give the benefit of the doubt. Compassion occurs when we can honestly ask this question of ourselves: "Have I ever done anything like that in my life?"

Using compassion, we can see when another is not coming from a good place. When we offer compassion, intimacy increases. Our partners feel safe with us, knowing we can show forgiveness.

When Zack arrived home two hours late with an uptight look on his face, Kristin sensed immediately that something was wrong.

She thoughtfully saved her request about her car needing to be replaced for another time and offered understanding, empathy, and nurturing. It turned out that Zack had been demoted. The new manager, lacking in emotional intelligence, had publicly announced his decision to move Zack to another position, effectively humiliating him in front of his team. Zack said it had been one of the most embarrassing and difficult days he had ever experienced. Kristin was able to help him at a time when he needed it most, as her compassion strengthened and added depth to their bond.

> *If you want other to be happy, practice compassion. If you want to be happy, practice compassion.*
>
> —Dalai Lama

Compromise

The divorce rate is catastrophically high for those who marry at a young age. This is due largely to the fact that when we are young, our identities are not well formed. We are still learning who we are and what our values are. We are learning how to express ourselves from the heart as well as the head. We are still figuring out what our priorities and needs are. Part of the maturing process is being willing to listen when someone is expressing his or her feelings or needs to us. We need to be respectful, attentive, and empathetic to what the other person is saying. When we have patience and show kindness and interest in our partner, these behaviors are almost always mirrored back to us. In this way, we can have an authentic and productive conversation regarding both sets of needs and wants. In understanding what both people need to feel satisfied, we will choose to cooperate or compromise with one another.

In healthy relationships, both partners feel valued and cherished. Both feel relieved and uplifted when they share their feelings, wants, and needs with one another. We understand how important it is to be honest about what we are thinking, desiring, and feeling. The skills of listening well, validating our partners' feelings, and showing compassion and support go a long way toward compromising when there is a clash of needs.

When we are truly present and have learned effective communication skills, we will be able to create emotional intimacy. We need to look at our loved one with eyes of appreciation, knowing that in times of conflict, we can both arrive at a win-win solution by seeking the middle ground while listening with respect to the other person's feelings and values.

When we can look at a situation not only from our point of view but also from our partners' point of view, we are on the road to reaching an acceptable agreement. During times when we want different outcomes, it is beneficial to remember that compromise is essential. Oftentimes, couples will argue ad infinitum. This reminds me of two attorneys arguing a case in a courtroom. Each one cites important stats and presents data from studies, hell-bent on winning the case. In my many years as a relationship coach, I have seen all too often couples fighting to be right, with both partners digging their heels in and arguing for their way. Each wants to win—but at the other's expense. The result is that the relationship is damaged.

Demanding only one solution creates resentments along with higher and higher levels of mistrust. In these situations, the loser thinks, *You don't care about me; you only care about yourself.* The winner thinks, *It's like pulling teeth. I'm angry that I wasted so much time fighting. He [or she] doesn't really care about what I want anyway.*

Resentments are like termites. They eat away at the foundation of trust and closeness. Therefore, win-lose situations are really lose-lose situations, as the one who caved in is left with festering resentments either consciously or unconsciously. He or she will get even. Therefore, the game is not over!

There are some who will say, "Okay," to almost any situation. They are the conflict avoiders. Since they want peace at any price, they will go out of their way to avoid an argument. They will roll their eyes, release their frustrations through loud sighs, or make sarcastic or funny comments. They might even make derogatory remarks about their partners. This passive-aggressive behavior often presents by their showing up late time after time, forgetting important dates and agreements, and so on. This causes harmful distance between the partners, which will grow and grow like a piece of yeast in a dark, moist place.

However, when partners choose to implement emotional intelligence and use maturity, kindness, and respect, this approach serves as a reassurance that their intention is to work out an acceptable compromise. After all, the goal is for each person to feel supported, loved, and cared about. The message is "I want you to be happy, sweetie, but I also want to be happy. I cherish our relationship and know we will work out an acceptable way to compromise."

> In every relationship, there are two halves of that relationship. Of those halves, you are only responsible for your half. It doesn't matter how close you think you are, or how strongly you think you love. There is no way you can be responsible for what is inside another person's head. When we try to be responsible for the other half, the result is a war of control. We have a choice. We can create a war of control or we can become a playmate and a team player. Playmates and team players play together, but not against each other. If you see your partnership as a team, everything will start to improve. In a relationship, as in a game, it's not about winning or losing. You are playing because you want to have fun. Generosity, freedom and love will create the most beautiful relationship; an ongoing romance.
> —Don Miguel Ruiz, *The Mastery of Love*

Commitment

What does it mean to be in a committed relationship? To what extent is commitment important?

You are fortunate when you are part of a fulfilling and beneficial relationship, something you truly value and cherish. When you are willing to make your relationship your top priority, you realize that your life is enhanced and made better. Happiness is best shared; you feel a sense of deep appreciation and enjoy expressing it to your partner and others. When you freely commit 100 percent, you show to yourself and your partner that your relationship is a treasure. Also, when you participate 100 percent in your relationship, you will find that you are never bored!

There are some who have a problem with committing fully. During times of stress and conflict, these partners turn away from one another, looking in opposite directions, rather than turning toward each other, sharing their feelings and their goals. For example, they might turn to others with their dissatisfaction rather than choosing to share and repair.

A common way of turning away from your partner is to escape into the arms of another. Affairs and other distractions serve to avoid dealing with the marital issues rather than confronting them. Many choose to distance themselves from the relationship issues by numbing themselves with work, gambling, drugs, sex, food, and alcohol. The list goes on.

Think of a small fire. We need to acknowledge that action must be taken; otherwise, the fire will spread and become destructive. Instead of putting out the fire, many people seek distractions outside their relationships, similar to Nero fiddling while Rome burns. The result is that issues cannot be resolved, and the distance grows wider and wider between the couple.

When a relationship becomes troubled, some fear being alone so much that they prepare for the worst in their minds. Their fear of being alone is so great that they begin warming up another in the bullpen. This preemptive behavior prevents them from the terror of having to go it alone. Rather than facing their abandonment issues (loneliness and anxiety), they bounce from relationship to relationship. They take no time for self-reflection, no time to heal their emotions, and no time to discover what *they* contributed to the dissolution of the partnership. They avoid the pain of being with themselves because they truly don't love who they are. Additionally, they have issues with being vulnerable, being close, and resolving conflict.

I refer to these commitment-phobes as entering a relationship with only one foot in and one hand on the doorknob. They are always expecting relationships to fail. Instead of being capable of a complete relationship, they are only capable of a partial relationship. This pattern will be repeated as they jump from one partner to another. Fear prevents them from being fully committed.

I have known couples who will threaten, "I am out of here! I've had it! My best days were before I met you!" They are frustrated and use these threats as a way of intimidating the other, doing so with some frequency. They will threaten divorce at the drop of a hat, saying, "Well, then let's just end this thing and go our separate ways!"

Toxic threats do irreparable damage to the foundation of trust and respect in a relationship. The recipient of these threats becomes defensive and erects huge, impenetrable walls. Once these destructive words have been put out there, they cannot be retracted. There is no psychological eraser that can take away the pain, devastation, mistrust, hurt, and anger these words cause.

To create a healthy relationship, it is essential to reassure your partner of your deep commitment to making the relationship healthy, successful, and mutually satisfying. As you show faith in the relationship and love for your partner and are comfortable with saying, "I'm sorry; I love you and want to work this out," during the most trying of times, your partner will reflect that back. Together you will experience the gratification (emotional, psychological, physical, and spiritual) of being part of a loving, committed relationship in which each partner feels secure, loved, and cherished.

Research has borne out that the happiest couples who experience long-term success in their relationships are those who are deeply committed to maintaining the emotional health of the relationship. They appreciate their partners and enjoy communicating this appreciation. They remember that honesty is imperative in a truly committed relationship; it is the only foundation on which trust can be built.

> **Mature love is composed and sustaining; a celebration of commitment, companionship, and trust.**
> —H. Jackson Brown Jr.

Commitment means to

- have a high-quality, deeply satisfying relationship;
- make the relationship a priority;
- know the value of showing appreciation and respect for one another's feelings, dreams, values, needs, and goals;
- be willing to admit when you've made a mistake and say, "I'm sorry; please forgive me";
- be willing to make it up to your partner when you've done or said something out of line;

- tell your partner how special he or she is and how much you love him or her;
- reassure your partner that you are fully committed and that you believe he or she is precious;
- remind your partner that you are willing to do whatever it takes to work out differences;
- remind your partner how deeply you are devoted and how much you truly care about him or her;
- thank your partner for caring about you, being there for you, and being an asset in your life; and
- forgive and ask to be forgiven quickly, honestly, and sincerely.

> You need to make a commitment; and once you make it, then life will give you some answers.
> —Les Brown

Doreen Virtue, best-selling author, spiritual clairvoyant, and motivational speaker, states, "Our relationships can be our greatest teachers of spiritual lessons like patience, self-understanding, assertiveness, boundaries, and forgiveness. The rewards of Romantic Love are worth the journey through any challenge because Love truly does heal all."

After a breakup, it is beneficial to use this transitional time to take an inward journey. This is a golden opportunity to become empowered and to learn that you are worthy. During this time of uncoupling, take the time to look deeply within. This can be a time of quiet reflection and inner healing. Self-reflection will lead to a deeper understanding of who you are and what you need to be happy. It is necessary to understand yourself without judgment and without blame. This leads to self-compassion, which leads to self-acceptance. Ultimately, the love you feel for yourself will be unconditional love. Treat yourself the way you would want your beloved to treat you. Apply exquisite self-care in your life. If you have a wounded self, it will preclude your capacity for experiencing love and intimacy in a healthy relationship.

Letting go of old resentments, blame, judgments, guilt, and self-pity will open the way to fully grieve. (Many under-estimate how important it is to grieve.) Grief is the way we manage change. However, it is necessary to feel your grief fully. Losses and endings are about change and surrender. We surrender so we are able to move forward and realize the joy of a new beginning. Remember that crisis also means opportunity. Focus on healing your heart as you make way for new opportunities to appear in your life. Things happen for a reason and a purpose.

> *Each relationship you have with another person reflects the relationship you have with yourself.*
> —Alice Deville

Intimate relationships are created when partners are able to be vulnerable—this means opening up their hearts and souls to one another. Many people, however, put up protective shields—layers and layers of defense. After a while, they lose touch with their true authentic selves as well as their feelings. Mistrust will not allow intimacy to exist. This book will help readers to be completely authentic with their loved ones.

The more we disclose about ourselves, the more our partners will mirror that disclosure back to us, feeling safe to be open. When we feel safe, we can be totally transparent and share our feelings, wants, and needs. We can honestly communicate about what we want from one another. Showing compassion and empathy establishes a healthy climate of trust, respect, safety, and caring. Dr. Harriet Lerner, in her famous book *The Dance of Connection*, writes, "The more intimate and enduring the relationship, the greater the longing to find some way to share our full selves, and the greater the consequences of not telling, of not being real." When we feel confident and are authentic, we enjoy sharing *all* our feelings and dreams. To develop vulnerability, we need the skill to be able to speak from the heart. In this way, we create a deep, rich, and satisfying relationship that has at its foundation a strong and meaningful friendship. Researchers have discovered that in healthy, fulfilling, successful relationships, each partner has a deep appreciation for the other. Additionally, both choose to focus on what's good about the relationship rather than on what might be lacking. They not only appreciate their partners—and frequently share their feelings—but also speak in loving, positive terms, letting their partners know how much they adore them.

> Intimacy means that we're safe enough to reveal the truth about ourselves in all its creative chaos. If a space is created in which two people are totally free to reveal their walls, then those walls, in time, will come down.
>
> —Marianne Williamson

To have a healthy, intimate relationship, you must have a whole, integrated, authentic self. To do this, you must do the following:

- Complete your healing. Close the door on the old relationship to make room for the new one.
- Give up the illusion of romantic and idealistic love. When we do, we will have realistic expectations; we understand the difference between lust and love.
- Develop a deep level of respect as well as introspection, which allows you to understand the unique and deserving person you have become. Through this awareness, you will be able to accept the lovable and beautiful person you know you are.
- Discover and embrace your new identity. We get clear about our values and are confident when we communicate them.
- Practice excellent self-care. The way you treat yourself will be reflected back to you time and time again. Begin the journey of excellent self-care. Learn to love and accept yourself in the present moment. We treat ourselves the way we would want our partner to treat us. We nurture ourselves continuously, realizing that self-care and self-love are paramount to living an extraordinary life. We are proactive about

the self-nurturing decisions we make, taking action and increasing our self-esteem every day. We value me time and enjoy spending time in our new beautiful company.

- Be still. Listen to the wise and persistent inner voice. This is the voice of intuition. It's your small yet powerful voice that will guide you. It wants you to speak the truth. It wants your highest good.
- Be sure to get enough sleep. Be sure to carve out enough time for inner reflection. By building a relationship with yourself, you will create satisfaction, joy, gratitude, and hope.
- Sit on a park bench or sit in your backyard. Close your eyes and give yourself me time. This is the beginning of self-care. Change your mind about doing. This is the new you, the one focused on being.
- As you practice loving, uplifting self-care, your life will improve radically on the inside as well as the outside.
- Trust your intuition as well as yourself.
- Understand and implement the law of attraction. Using daily affirmations keeps us centered and positive. We understand that our thoughts create our reality. When we change our thoughts, we change our reality. Positive thoughts will raise our vibrational frequency.

- Be clear that the way you feel about yourself is crucial to being a part of a healthy, happy, and fulfilled relationship. When you are filled with love, respect, and kindness, you will have more to share with others, and your relationships will blossom.
- Process your difficult feelings and regain your self-confidence. The way we feel about ourselves is crucial to being a part of a healthy, happy, mutually beneficial relationship. Loving ourselves unconditionally results in attracting loving, compassionate, authentic, caring people to show up in our lives. After all, they mirror the exact vibration we are emitting.
- Go ahead: fall in love with yourself.

> *To love oneself is the beginning of a life-long romance*
>
> Oscar Wilde

I hope that you have enjoyed your journey through and that many of the situations and circumstances resonated with you. There are many factors that affect who we are and how we relate to others. And, when it comes to love, which is one of the strongest and most precious emotions we have, who we are becomes key to finding a positive outcome.

As I stated in the beginning of the book, my goal is to help you find the love you are seeking by having a clear understanding of what might have gone awry in your former relationship. In any relationship it takes both parties to make it good or sabotage it.

When you understand that the only thing in life that you can control is YOU, then the whole process becomes somewhat easier. You are a wonderful, lovable person who deserves all the love you **desire**! Always begin with you.

> Let the love in your heart be first for you.
> Then all other loves will be richer
> And you will reap the rewards you desire
> and deserve.
>
> M.J.Waldock

1. **The way you feel about yourself is crucial to a happy, healthy and fulfilled relationship. Loving ourselves unconditionally results in attracting loving, compassionate, authentic, caring people to show up in our lives. You are energy and others reflect back the exact vibration you are emitting.**

You will have more to share with others and your relationship will blossom.

2. Feelings don't need to be explained but they do need to be processed. Processing your difficult feelings will help you regain your self confidence.

3. Forgive yourself and others. Forgiveness relieves you of guilt, shame, disappointment and a host of other emotions. Forgiveness opens the door to many new experiences. Do it, it's important.

4. Acceptance is key. No one is perfect and therefore perfection is a myth. Although self-improvement is always good, feeling that you are less than perfect can only cause you to dislike yourself. The first step to self-love is acceptance.

5. Grieving. The loss of anything important in life causes grief. Don't run away from it; acknowledge it and let it take its course. Seek help as you are going through the process and be ready to let go. The past can no longer serve you except when you learn a lesson from what happened.

> *When we learn from all our relationships, how can there be any such thing as a bad relationship?*
>
> —*Dr. Susan Jeffers*

Thank you for taking this journey. I am confident now that you are more self-aware and have learned that you are not to blame for whatever failure you feel that you had;, you are ready to love again.

Manifest the love you desire. Envision it; write it down and truly believe that the universe will bring it to you. You will attract that which you are truly seeking.

LOVE BIG, LOVE BOLD, LOVE HARD and ABOVE ALL – LOVE YOU UNCONDITIONALLY!

Acknowledgments

I am enormously grateful for the many, many beautiful people who supported me as well as contributed to my book. I wish to acknowledge the many kind, loving and supportiveng people who provided me inspiration, motivation and courage. There are too many to name. Please forgive me for not including each and every name: the list would simply go on and on.

A very special thank you to Sharon Bornheimer who has been a special and loving angel in my life. For without her unwavering encouragement along with her writing and editing talents, I would not have completed this book. I am truly blessed to have her in my life.

I am especially grateful to my very dear friend Marlene Waldock. Her enthusiastic and steadfast belief in me brought this book to life. I truly appreciate her kindness, brilliance and devotion to my work. Marlene has enhanced my life in more ways than I can articulate. I am blessed by our friendship.

I want to thank my longtime and cherished friend, Dr. Nikki Conte, who has been an inspiration to me in my writing. She has always had a steadfast belief in me and is one of the most compassionate and loving people on the planet.

I want to acknowledge my dear friend, LoAnne Mayer, who also inspired me countless times during the writing of my book. Having authored a bests-selling book herself, she was always there to encourage, guide and support me. She is an absolutely accomplished, caring and amazing woman.

Thank you Jodi Topitz; your commitment to excellence, your talents, love and support have been invaluable assets to me.

I would like to thank my dear friend, Amanda Borghese, who always believed in me and who supported the need for a book that would help others to let go, learn, and move forward. Her enthusiasm, encouragement and wisdom have meant the world to me and I am truly grateful!

A very special thank you goes to the many wonderful and dedicated people on the staff at Balboa Press. I thank you for helping me, guiding me and assisting me in this labor of love. I truly appreciate you traveling with me on this exciting journey.

I have been truly blessed by having three sons and a daughter and two bonus daughters. I thank you all from the bottom of my heart for your unwavering love, patience, input and encouragement.

I am deeply grateful to my beloved husband Steve who never once complained while we postponed our fun weekend plans for me to work on the book. Thank you for your love, support and belief in my work. You have nurtured me and pushed me. I cherish you, my wonderful husband and best friend.

A heartfelt thank you to my clients to whom I dedicate this book. I feel both honored and privileged to have coached you. Thank you for sharing your trials and triumphs ; your learning experiences and allowing me to be there for you. You have been my greatest teachers over the years. I feel both honored and privileged to have coached you!

CPSIA information can be obtained
at www.ICGtesting.com
Printed in the USA
BVHW072330040119
537091BV00003B/43/P